Oedipus is Innocent

Oedipus is Innocent

Selected poems of Nicolas Calas

Edited and translated by Lena Hoff

Smokestack Books
1 Lake Terrace, Grewelthorpe, Ripon HG4 3BU
e-mail: info@smokestack-books.co.uk
www.smokestack-books.co.uk

Copyright Lena Hoff &
Louisiana Museum of Modern Art,
Humlebæk, Denmark

Translations copyright,
Lena Hoff, 2020

ISBN 9781916139275

Smokestack Books
is represented by
Inpress Ltd

Preface

My relationship with Nicolas Calas dates back to 1999 when I organised his personal papers, manuscripts and letters for what was to become The Nicolas and Elena Calas Archives at the Danish Institute at Athens. Since then I have dedicated the major part of my scholarly life to the study of Calas. A Master's thesis was followed by a Ph.D. on his cultural politics, later turned into the intellectual biography *Nicolas Calas and the Challenge of Surrealism* (Copenhagen: Museum Tusculanum Press 2014) the Greek publications of his correspondence with the Trotskyist Michalis Raptis (Pablo) and Calas' *Surrealism and the Making of History* (Athens: Agra Publications 2002 and 2016). I began translating the poems while writing the biography and soon discovered that the translation process became a way of understanding his poems more fully and deeply. While the time has perhaps not yet arrived to publish his collected poems in translation, I have instead attempted to make a representative choice of some of his most well-known and characteristic poems which cover his entire life-span and show his intriguing development as a poet.

Lena Hoff

Contents

Introduction	13
Poems (1933)	
The Song of the Harbour Works	21
Demonstration	25
Acropolis	31
Imprisoned	33
Reading History Books	36
Round Symphony	40
Harbour	45
Erotic	47
Santorini	50
Columns of the Temple of Olympian Zeus	55
Minoan	56
Notebooks (1933–1936)	
Revolution	63
Athens 1933	66
Narcissus 1934	67
Pre-Myth	68
Contract with Demons	70
When the Eyes Last No Longer	74
The French Poems (1937–1940)	
To Travel Out of the Past	79
The Agony in the Crowd	80
The Ruins of a City	81
The Massacre of the Innocent	82
In a Time Still Unfinished	83
Song of Oblivion	84
The Dance of the Survivors	86
The Blue of the Dream	87
The Storm at Dawn	88
The Great Misunderstood	89
Oedipus is Innocent	90
Narcissus in the Desert	91

Torn from Mirrors	92
Starless Departure	94
In the Glare of the Gestures	96
Here Lies the Heart	97
Very Long Hours	98
Spartans	99

Unpublished American Poems (1952–1953)
Before the night fades...	103
Corruptions	104
The Island	105
Togetherness	106

Nikitas Randos Street (1963–1977)
Foreign Vessels	109
With Kisses	110
Heroi(n)sm	111
Man of Two Races	112
Storm of Misfortune	113
'Man of foreign race...'	114
Melina, queen of my Sundays...	115
Mockery	116
Sweet-Kissing Aspasia	117
Happy City	118
In the Isles of Byron and Sappho...	119
No and Never	120
'There is no answer...'	121
We want no absolution...	122
Past happenings are blooming...	123
I received the Acropolis...	124
I engage in allusions and illusions...	125
When your heart misses a beat...	126
The fare from Athens to Nova York...	127
The Back of the Hare	128
I cultivated a closed garden...	129
Regime of allusions and precision...	130
Structure and breath the poem...	131
The wind-swept branches of Pennsylvania...	132

Scripture and Light (1977–1982)
   Second Book   135
   Kneeling Descendant   137
   Falling Stars   138
   Younger because he innovates...   140
   Godless only the Hermaphrodite... 141
   The Day after Yesterday   142

Last American Poems (1979–1982)
   Black is Beautiful   145
   Four o'clock   146
   Who Speaks?   148
   Xmas = 125th Street   150

Notes   151
Acknowledgements   157

Introduction

Nicolas Calas (1907–1988) is a fascinating case of a singular poet in constant search of change and modernity. His intellectual and artistic restlessness led him to constantly experiment with new ways of expressing his ideas on the nature of art and poetry, ethics and politics, seeking to uncover the hypocrisy of capitalist society and middle-class morality. Calas' poetry is, first and foremost, characterised by its multiple transformations and playful experimentations. His emphasis on the criticality of all artistic expression brought a highly unique sense of sharpness and intellectualism to his poems through their challenging propositions and multiple transfigurations. Furthermore, Calas leaves a trail from Athens to New York, via sojourns in Paris and Lisbon, which reveals a truly international poet and polemicist, writing in Greek, French and English.

The cosmopolitanism of Calas was the natural result of his upbringing. He was born Nikos Kalamaris in 1907 in Lausanne, Switzerland, but grew up in Athens, the only son of Ioannis Kalamaris who descended from a family of ship-owners and landowners from Syros, and Rosa Caradja who was the great-granddaughter of Markos Botsaris, the military leader and hero of the Greek War of Independence. Calas' wealthy bourgeois background meant that he received a solid education in French and English by private tutors which laid the foundation for his broad knowledge of foreign literary trends. However, his socialist awakening in the 1920s, following the refugee crisis in the wake of the Asia Minor catastrophe of 1922, also put him in conflict with his own social class and his family and created an unbridgeable gap with his father.

Calas first became involved with Marxist politics through the radical Student Society while he was a student of Law and Political Science at the University of Athens in the late 1920s. During the 1930s Calas was a frequent columnist and critic in a string of Athenian left-wing and literary periodicals under the pseudonym M. Spieros (in homage to the French revolutionary Maximilien Robespierre) writing on a wide range of topics such as cinema, literature, art and politics. Making his mark during these years as a critic and polemicist, he came to advocate a new cultural politics of the Left inspired mainly by Surrealism, Futurism, Trotsky and Freudo-Marxism – a radical poetics which naturally also supplied the framework for his own poetry.

He made his debut as a poet in 1933 with the publication of *Poems* under another assumed name – Nikitas Randos. The collection showed a wide variety of literary styles, including Futurism, Expressionism and Symbolism. Calas' highly idiosyncratic way of using his poems as a form of experimental work-shop, playing with his sources of inspiration at the same time as trying to formulate something entirely new, continued in the four *Notebooks*, the small poetry collections that circulated privately *hors de commerce* in Athens between 1933 and 1936.

In his first Futurist phase Calas showed a clear influence by Mayakovsky when investigating the city of Athens through the use of a fast rhythm (mostly created with quite short forward-pushing lines), linguistic experimentations and neologisms which expressed his socialist thought and revolutionary goals. One of Calas' most famous poems, 'Round Symphony', describes the soulless life of Omonia square in central Athens determined by 'pounds, shillings and pence' forcing its inhabitants to remain enslaved in an endless circular movement. Another poem from Calas' futurist phase, 'The Song of the Harbour Works' is situated in a concrete-covered harbour and describes the hardships of the dockers and their exploitation from the hands of a cynical boss in league with the gold-diggers of Wall Street.

The most important artistic movement for Calas' poetic development was undoubtedly Surrealism – an ambitious undertaking which set out on an adventurous journey in search of revolution and dream, social action and the unconscious, the marvellous and *amour fou*. The explorations of the unconscious documented through their poetic experimentations aimed for a total liberation on all fronts. Calas began taking an interest in Surrealism very early on but it took a few years before he became a surrealist himself and his poems showed a clear influence by the French movement. The fourth and final poetry *Notebook,* from November 1936, contained his first attempt at a surrealist poem, 'Contract with Demons' as well as what could be called a declaration of surrealist faith entitled 'Pre-Myth' before the separately published 'When the Eyes Last No Longer' in 1937 revealed his total immersion in surrealist poetics.

While Calas' avant-garde poetry was received with suspicion and downright hostility by his communist friends who advocated the doctrine of socialist realism, his socialist convictions put him in opposition to the dominant forces in Greek criticism which responded mostly negatively to his poems. Calas' ensuing ideological and artistic isolation made it difficult for him to stay in Greece and after the fascist coup and instalment of General Metaxas in August 1936 it became necessary to leave. While he had already split his time between Greece and France for a couple of years, he now moved permanently to Paris, where he joined the Surrealist group gathered around its charismatic and undisputed leader André Breton. Continuing to write poems in both Greek and French he also published the highly polemical Freudo-Marxist theoretical work *Foyers d'incendie* under his new pseudonym Nicolas Calas in 1938. At this time the French surrealists had turned to Trotskyism and when Breton went to visit the exiled Trotsky in Mexico, where they formulated a joint manifesto 'Towards a Free Revolutionary Art', he brought Calas' book with him as a gift.

After his move to Paris, Calas turned to an increasingly surrealist poetic expression. In fact, the group of poems that he wrote in French between 1937 and 1940 (unpublished at the time) are his only poems than can be characterised as surrealist through and through. The surrealists emphasised tension, conflict and what was understood to be the necessary shock to jolt man from passivity and complacency into revolt and change. In Calas' French poems the motif of fire symbolised transformation and the revolutionary forces, while water, often represented by Narcissus, symbolised the static and nostalgia. Narcissus must die in order for new forces to emerge and the all-important metamorphosis to occur. The result of this transformation, later described as a new Prometheus, was Calas' idea of the defiant poet who challenges oppressive society and who revolts against the tyrant and his henchmen.

After the outbreak of the Second World War he was forced to leave Paris since a new decree law denied foreigners residing in France the right to political asylum. After a four-months sojourn in Lisbon, arranging his escape from a war-torn Europe, he finally made it to New York in the beginning of 1940 as one of the first emigre surrealists. Right away he was invited to contribute to the avant-garde journal *View* and also edited a surrealist anthology for the 1940 *New Directions* literary journal and thus helped pave the way for surrealism in America.

Before eventually carving a niche for himself as an art critic and lecturer in New York, he earned his living from a number of odd jobs. From 1942 he worked in the French and Greek sections of the Office of War Information as well as in the Balkan section of the Intelligence Service. In 1943 he married Elena von Hoershelman, a Russian-born psychoanalyst with whom he would go on to collaborate on a number of research projects, such as anthropological studies with Margaret Mead, and his later studies of Hieronymus Bosch. It was not until the 1950s, when he briefly returned to Greece, that Calas again started writing poems in Greek. Almost all of these new poems were written in the satirical vein. The disillusionment of his 'home-coming' visits proved decisive for Calas' poetic development as a satirist. He later talked of being utterly disappointed by 1950's Greece and described Athens as a suffocating place.

Although Calas' poems from this period were markedly different stylistically as well as in temperament, there are also many similarities to be found with his earlier poems. The sharp satire and biting irony, mostly accomplished through elaborate puns and multi-level connotations, were clearly new features. However, the critical mind and the intellectualism which underlie the poems have much in common with the Calas of the 1930s. Some of the most biting (and funny) satires mocked the literary establishment and Greek conservative modernists, such as the Nobel Laureate George Seferis, post-war Americanised petit-bourgeois Greeks, and Greece as a tourist destination. Other favoured targets for Calas' were religion, the royal family and, after the military coup of 1967, the rule of the colonels.

Most of the satires are written in an immensely dense language characterised by cryptic word-games and some of them are almost overloaded with puns, deliberate misspellings to denote double meanings, and sometimes caricatures which border on the grotesque. Although the punning style of the satires almost defies any attempt at translation, I have tried to keep some of their playful character apart from providing the reader with detailed footnotes which include both linguistic explanations as well as reminders of the historical, political and cultural background for these poems.

Calas' use of a satirical form later gave way to a different kind of poetic expression in the mid-1970s, which can be divided into two groups. Firstly, a poetry of poetics and secondly, a self-referential or reflective poetry. He identified himself with the prodigal son, the outcast and the hermaphrodite, and opposed confession with revelation. As Calas got older his poems reveal a need to explain himself to a new Greek audience unfamiliar with the poet of the 1930s. His last poetic phase thus became an attempt to connect the poet of the past, Nikitas Randos, with the poet of the present, Nicolas Calas.

Calas remained largely forgotten or unknown in Greece until the mid-1960s when his satirical poems appeared in the literary avant-garde journal *Pali*. Then came the 1977 poetry collection *Nikitas Randos Street* which consisted of the four 1930's *Notebooks* and his 1960's and 1970's satirical poems prefaced by Odysseas Elytis. The book won him the Greek State Prize for Poetry, spawning new interest in his work. The jury's explanatory statement for rewarding Calas especially emphasised the innovative, playful and ground-breaking aspect of these poems: 'He accomplishes a poetry that has, existing within and beyond the dogma of any school, an inherent density in its succession of continuity, its spark, its intellectual base and its surprise: that is, all the characteristics of a modernistic poetry.'

Calas consequently started visiting Greece again on a regular basis. His early Greek essays were collected and republished and in 1983 another collection of poems called *Scripture and Light* came out comprising his 1932 debut collection as well as poetry written between 1977 and 1983. After his death in 1988 Calas' reputation in Greece has been steadily growing. However, in the English-speaking world he remains largely unknown and, above all, untranslated, something that this book seeks to amend.

Lena Hoff, 2020

**Poems
(1933)**

The Song of the Harbour Works

I saw them disembowel the sea
and the sea give birth to people
but the pain was theirs
theirs alone and quite terrifying
I felt it in the noise of the fish
and in the silence of the workers
I felt it
in the iron prayers
triangulating the sky
– and isn't also the eye of God within a triangle? –
I felt it in the entreating voices of men
inviting all holy men to carnal acts
and her
who if she would live today – the others
who say their Sunday prayers
would have done it
– that is how far their impiety stretches
Miss Palestine.

I even saw them dig up the sea
flooding it
with slabs of concrete
– the squaring of pain –
thus displacing the water
that gold-diggers drink greedily
in the City of Wall Street –
gulping down that hardened liquid
the hot ice
yellowed from the urine
of kidneys
ruthlessly exploited by labour.

Not everything here is made of gold though
nothing is made of gold around here
just the sun
but the sun is far away
or the sand
which doesn't belong to them either
but these are the colours
that the son of Noah sees here.

Blue is the sky
what could possibly cause it pain?
Black though is the earth
from the coal being unloaded
black are the lips of the people
unloading the black earth
and when they go to bed at night
to wear themselves out through pleasure
black all will be black
and the heart of the boss
wrapped in fat
– the fat keeps him warm –
when he drives by in a Packard
that also looks black
under the orders
and turn the others white –
I have also seen it
merely giving orders
chewing on his Havana
devouring the hopes of so many others –
I left – deafened
by the noise of the smoke
coming out of his mouth.

But, wherever I turned my eye
I heard voices
the voices of poverty building hills
made to spew up filthy houses
thrown together one on top of one another
as in a whorehouse –
this is where the workers live – those who belong to the sector
of the great harbour works.

Elsewhere other voices –
warehouses furrowed by loud commands
kissing bodies that do not want them
and sensuous roads extensions of the works
are thrown into the ships
where the half-naked bodies of the workers
when sweetly warmed by the sun
exhaust themselves during the hours of rest
lighting candles to Aphrodite.

It is a terrifying image
all the barges brimming with yearning
choking the sea
which leaves for another destination far away from people
seeking there its waves.

They are building a new land here
the foundations of the manager's parquet floor
and of the many shares of different companies –
iron forests are rising
horrible though is the bird-song
of so many freighter whistles.

Just like the cats in my yard
madly chasing each other
the cars are looking for work
and their songs
are no less erotic.

'Buy Shell Petrol'
it is written on a house in the twelfth precinct
this is the language spoken around here
the poetry of the harbour
from where you cannot see the sea
and only the burbling of the silo can be heard
this is the poetry I love
telling me all that moves me
it is the song of cities
where people suck the condensed milk
of a mother
only God could have made a mother.

Demonstration

Osram bulb candles at night on healthy streets
plenty of candles in the churches
radio transmitters
equal in the eyes of God and the rest of them
but now at two in the afternoon
with the power of thousands of candles
the voices of the masses of demonstrators
expand the street
the flames are castrated no more
they castrate in churches and palaces
but here they burn
the commands of courts
and from their ashes
the hopes of the workers –
it has not been in vain then
the copulation of so many plans

'Forty centuries have their eyes on us'
the great and victorious General said to his troops
Bonaparte
we, on the other, hand, don't know how many years that are watching us
how could we know it since we have no emperor
what we feel
is
that we have fetters
that must go
because they hurt
because they are too tight, squeezing
like the fingers
clenched together
in the shape of a fist
the empty palm
must cover its nakedness
squeezing

the crowds are squeezing
like the cat
before jumping
as soon as we jump –
but listen up now
from behind your closed windows
closed in honour of us
the erotic mewing:
we fell in love with power.

The streets have grown narrower
like our exhilaration
which has widened
its cries filling the sky
smothered with aeroplanes
which we now lift up high
with our enormous body –
the crowd grows larger
and the masses of people
like a sewer
where the water of others is poisonous
because it burst making their anger explode
their anger
our anger
and that anger
that anger
now flows
it flows
slowly
forcefully
swiftly
it flows
and no one stops to ask
where it will take us.

And sweeter still than the sweetest flesh
is the scent of our demands
hurled with the battle cries
at the masses
from the mouths of the speakers
the canons watching us like cyclops
inhale their echo
before the rocks tumble down

Suddenly
nobody knows why yet
we are running
as a waterfall we run up the streets
we kiss their shape
black and white
from all directions black and white
and our long body
licking the white walls –
against our will
the crows are flying low now.

The streets are calling us
they swallow our anger
the long streets are shouting
and this barking
surges horribly into our ears
toads, crows, dogs together with sirens –
how it skins our life
all this hearing of the voices
from the scurry in the street
inconceivably horrifying
the voices carrying
unfriendly
deadly kisses –
the ghost of death
throws a ghastly light
on the rash faint-hearted
people in flight.

Everywhere all around us we see only streets
in front of us and then
to our right and left are streets
broad streets, narrow, with tram tracks
with asphalt and without asphalt
everything in the city is indifferent
the harrowing grin
the sarcastic smile
of a mouth
its voice can now be heard
by our ears alone.

We try in vain to escape the companionship of bullets
arrangement of horizontal lines
streets, lead, people
whoever said that parallels meet in infinity
here they are joined
and here is not infinity
but the works of man
even if they are so horribly disguised
nobody notices their masks anymore
in the dance of madmen they sometimes fall
the music is enough
and the street organ of those with money
plays a mad game with us
to its sound
we jump
newly fallen bodies
forever fallen.

Where is the police constable
in order to regulate
the circulation of blood
on the pavements of arteries?
The blood
the red mark
of a city that coquettishly tried to kill us
the red mark

the make-up
concealing
weak streets
after the dispersal
of the workers'
demonstration.

After the dispersal
of so many workers
how sweet the air is
slowly slowly doors are opened
and windows
look, even Juliet on the balcony
with her mother
'order has been restored'
and as for our own agitation
the blood-letting that took place
will appease us.

I remember a child's head
that had been trampled
afterwards
it took up a lot of space
the brain, the eyes, the blood
strange
I wonder if it takes a lot of imagination
for someone to understand
the dimensions of the dead.

The usual voices of the street
can now be heard again
how great the silence must be
for all of this to be heard once again.

But in truth
sometimes the crowds are easily dispersed
like water turning into a river
evaporates with the rain
and the bullets open
drop by drop the hearts
and yet, it is no indiscretion
in times of censorship
it is better more drastic
for them not to write at all
to spill their inkstands
as for the stains
you simply blot them afterwards
with a few flowers in the graveyard.

Acropolis

In the foreground
the Parthenon
poisoned with Psycharian ink
false, dead
killed by a lens on deluxe paper
by Boissonnas
gravedigger of Greece –
in the background folded hands
twisted
in a posture of prayer
intense prayer
hands voluble fat
superbly fat
on the fingers instead of rings
electrical wires
vibrating the word
    Renan
– statesman of the Acropolis –
verger –
on top of the marbles
feet, belly, breasts, hands
dishevelled hair
of Delilah
but the locks shorn
she is a dancer who grew tired of parquet floors
and leaps
among old marbles
provocatively
leaps among columns
fantastically positioned
by that poet of great inspiration
Herr Karl Baedeker –
and all of this
the projectionist of some exhibition at Zappeion
advertising a French firm

banged sadistically
into our ears with punches
the ungodly is determined
to rhyme with the moon
while on moonlit nights
the tax-collector solicits the kisses
hidden under the skirt of a fake caryatid
and leaves them
with fat bellies
and others with tubes of six hundred and six
only cylinders can be seen around here
straight fallen columns
marble and others
roll-film, Agfa, Kodak
of coins – the change
exchanged from dollars and sterling
cylindrical also these words
falling juicily
words inspired
by the horror provoked
by the cannon-shots of Morosini
the cannons also cylindrical
each day they knock down acropolises
restored by others in negative plates
the clicks of Kodaks shout out
words recited
to the rhythm of an Adler automobile engine
madam actress
prostitutes our ears
with a weak larynx
sewer of her soul
finally spilling into
applause
– black foam of Venetian sea –

Imprisoned

I've grown weary of the books around me and my many
    notebooks
the walls surrounding my room
I want to immobilise them with words of concrete.

The walls are alive turning around and around in my room
the walls are alive turning until they reach deep inside my mind
the walls are alive and will not allow my words to spread
    out branches
they prune them and the corpses of my words are left behind
shrivelled up beings spread out on unlined paper
their smell cannot be heard even by the light of the lamp
obscuring all that I say underneath stones
the walls are alive while I live within walls
their touch makes me shudder
their endless gallop crowns my dizziness
they were perhaps more beautiful motionless stagnant
but they are more truthful when running with the speed of light
from Eden and beyond until now and even farther I'm afraid.

Faster still than the words the walls are raised
stopping the ink and making a pool out of the black
    surface of the words
while it should be gushing forth with the force of a waterfall
flooding the tyrannies hidden in masses with Byronic notes
tearing them down to their foundations
nowadays the poet cannot but envision Bastilles that fall
entire forests of towers even adorn the bottom
of vast calm waters with the anchors of despair
innumerable prisons are erected from the Sing Sing
    rocks of America
to the blue seas of Greece to the fortress of Izaddin
and from the Thames and the Danube and the Vistula
and from the lagoons of the Venetian canals
still hot the spray of sighs blows in
cultivated in the greenhouses of freedom.

Within infamous walls large numbers of soaking wet bodies rot away
where are you my Christ in this overflowing water
that encircle so many prisons
will you supply the dark colour of wounded bodies?
Only at nuptial parties the drunkenness of miracles is not worth it
we want no wine but black ink and red words
which colour the paper let it drink the desires of those
whose every syllable rhymes with stone
let the rhyming be destroyed with a mad but deeply human glance
and this psalm now sprout freely and unsuspecting
in street corners where the wind defies the walls
carrying the fragrance of flowers far
far away to gardens not yet cultivated.

That great day has not yet arrived though
and with machinery the penal servitude continues to enclose
    the earth with snake-like walls
fruit poisoned with gaols
the trains drag the convicts from prison to prison
and stop at stations of the world
where Pelasgic yesterday and with iron now grind down our desires.

From the pyramids graves for the hopes of slaves
from the hanging gardens where thorny blossoms sweetly smell
for the slaves the thorns
from the Roman palaces prisons for those who are left outside
from the Great Wall, from the embankments of China
the grievances of the damned rise up as a giant roar –
and today in the war underneath the earth
and at sea gigantic walls offer new tears
the walls cover the sky with endless tears
the walls of Babel which supplements the cypresses of the New World
graveyard guards where the poor are living with an electric
    chair for their throne
and from these infidel summits the voice of Zephyrus now
    gushes forth
singing with marble gateways on keys of synchronous structure
unbelievable stories – the work of people slaves of the stone

telling us how they lifted it high in pain
for it to breathe freely in the skies of time
while its enslaved poets breathe the tuberculosis on their slow walk.

See how the walls are racing racing
smashing the horizon flooding the earth
factories, palaces, theatres, museums, warehouses, clinics
London, Rome, Peking, Tokyo leave me indifferent
the walls are racing racing
with wheels of dollars and petrol from Mosul
leaving oil-stains – stages in the work progress
a rare sight, an international meeting
I wonder if my song will be able to set fire to the hearts in time
before the walls of my study will be covered in mould
the mouldiness of prison
the prison which locks up bodies
or the other one even more horrible with walls of despair?
I write so slowly and the readers pronounce so badly the ideas
that I am afraid to grow tired of seeing the others still being stationed.

No, the prison walls
will not hold my words
the wind will grab my papers
and throw them to the streets
scatter them
and even if they live far away from my soul
and I remain naked
I will have for a voice my fist.

Reading History Books

I allow being born inside of me
stories of yesterday and the day before yesterday
I made them live inside of me
a life of their own
so much a life of their own
that they were in pain and me with them
kicking me many years back in time
making me look in old mirrors
for imprints of the hopes of today –
this is how I spent many a day and night
then
puffy eyes
I closed them at the steps of time
but it was too late
in my darkness
street lamps were shining on the roads
where reflections of silence
projected all their secrets not yet burnt –
from the blazing history forgotten lives leapt up
throwing themselves at me
grasping my ravaged guts.

No matter if the book is small, big, heavy
it ignites it climbs
and there high up among the sparks
the many-coloured, the blue, the green
the white and the yellow
the deep crimson
I run –
that mottled fire
accompanies me
day and night in my dreams
like a crazed female jazz dancer
I run about, a dancer
among the shadows

cast by each flame
on the back of another –
the more I burn
the higher I jump
but that rhythm engulfed in flames
which follows me
how can I write it down
since it scorches the iambs
and the notes of the lyre
as if everything
was dedicated to
the terrible raging of the fire?
That fire
which an indescribable wind
Judaically gave to me –
as the days go by, the years
by a Promethean calendar
all the faster
the rhythm
of the wind's sparkle
and therefore
my dance –
I run with no rhythm
in the winds
with footsteps of fire –
they move all the more quickly
the playful warm lines
reach high
forcing me
to dance more boldly
I leap and jump
to the mad sounds
of a many-coloured fire
but wherever I tread
flames rise up again
their hot symphony
grows wider and wider
intoxicating celebration

covers my horizon
leaving
new horizons
luminously to emerge
within them
from ashes born again
warmer, crazier
the same but a new dance
with the same and other winds
with similar and different sparks
I see my awkward self
trying.

I now give birth to
fiery compositions
they demand life
which it pains me to give them
but which they nonetheless must have –
I wish for such tyrannical fires
that were lit for me
to extinguish them
with new flames –
I am the shower of sparks
of ever-burning pain
they will blow them further beyond
encircling lands
with dances that show the way to
night fishers with lanterns in the waters
and on land to the burning of the reaped fields –
the whole world must
become an enormous fire –
crippled then like Hephaestus
I will sit in a corner
I
in my room
showing the others how they dance around
with fires
that once

and still burn me ceaselessly
that which I fear though
– and in my most outrageous dreams
all is not warm sparkles –
perhaps the others
are
the many many others
they are unable to discern now
as also in the past
anything but thick thick smoke –
that is how I remember
some ugly history books
exceptionally hazy
like steamed up mirrors
that let you see
from smoky fires
only the smoke –
with which they are thickly thickly covered.

Round Symphony

It turns and turns dreadfully
the round street
they turn and turn dreadfully
in the round street
a thousand different people
machines of all kinds
turn and turn slowly
the lame, the blind and the old
the two-wheeled cart with the half-dead mule
the number three tram that stops close by
the yellow tram a reminiscence of a Belgian firm
turns and turns slowly
the prostitute on her beat
and the young homosexual
and behind the young man
a retired officer
hero of two victorious wars
ex-thug in Smyrna
turns and turns slowly
the child that doesn't like school
and the unemployed waiting for a job somewhere
crowds of people turning slowly
in the mornings at Omonia Square
lots of things turn slowly
all day long at the main square
small pieces of paper of all kinds
little rags that were perhaps once beautiful
and even dust swirls around slowly
and the phonograph record
slowly turns out an old tango
countless thoughts turn around
and around Omonia Square
occasionally they meet
on their circular path
before disappearing down a side street
together or separately

before disappearing into the earth –
the roads of the earth uniting Athens with Piraeus
offering the sea to some
– who can ever tell why they want the sea –
to others money, love
in Omonia Square they offer life
the crowds go out crop up with pain
ready to turn over like a ball
– which street will be, I wonder, the lucky number? –
The shoe-shiner calls out tickets for the Navy Lottery
he walks hurriedly around the great square
mannequins on a phonograph record
that shouts out *The Daily Telegraph* and *The National Herald*
the price of a tie sold at unemployment rates
pointed is the needle that grinds out the sounds
motivated by money
and the square turns
while the wretched people try to remain still
what pushes them on down there on earth
far from any air
what hopes or what horrible motive?
If only all these people
passing through Omonia at night
could stand still for a moment
and give life to the stones
if only the people could exchange
a few simple words
like human beings
and the lights roaring out their rich qualities
could be drowned with hearts –
and the buses stop for a moment
and even the wretched taxis take a rest
and the asphalt cease to suffer for a while
if only the square could be relieved from the pains of bodies
and *The Daily Telegraph* not appear for one day
let it be the turn of souls to wander freely
no matter if in a straight or a circular movement
around Omonia Square

let them turn in huge circles
in motionless and alien orbits –
and stop the phonograph from playing an old tango
how beautiful the great square then would be
when people will wear
even trees and the buses
how sweetly they will speak saying
all they had never thought
while rushing by
tripping on each other
the words will walk
they will create ....
what will they not create ....
.... in that general human harmony?
....
But alas!
Who disturbs today the circles
that disturb all of us
pounds, shillings and pence
make Omonia move on its axis
they swirl workers around the square like tops
and the rich, the poor and the poor
and in those diabolical swirls
the wind lifts up skirts
airing pleasure and pain
all of Athens can be found at Omonia
even the most secret desires live down there
the love which is paid for begins there
and the demonstrations for higher wages
there begins the dizziness
that makes you see everything as if turning around
I love naked squares like Omonia
they let you see every shadow
flung into the streets
and the stagnant muddied waters lie there in puddles
forming circles
houses are reflected in the puddles
the ugly houses of Omonia

two- and three-storeyed and higher still
strange are the houses of Omonia
they don't speak like other buildings
but who listens to what they say?
I'm truly sorry for them
they must feel terribly dizzy
from the record that turns all day
and prevents them from sleeping at night
just as the streets they are frightfully lit up
like champagne ignites penniless show-girls
the houses then also swirl around drunkenly
the entire square leaps
in this whirl
the houses leap up
blot out the sky
paint it black
and the round street supplies a rhythm
creating a sound crazier than any dance
in the cities behind so many layers of paint
worn by the night so as not to appear gloomy
dancing in so many circles so as to conceal the tedium of day
which forever wanders in memory
at night at two in the morning
Omonia spins around from too much wine
or too little food
revealing her soulless life to us
the silence that overflows her
the silence that surrounds our existence
and makes us dizzy
at the square scattered papers
weep their daily weariness
who knows if one day
these tears will not bring down the square
or perhaps in desperation from all the spinning around
she will decide some day at noon
to reflect the night sky
and in the midst of the black square
will we people find the edge of the circle?

The squares of every city
turn people and machines around like tops
In Athens, Omonia Square turns around
and in my mouth when I pronounce her name
the letters spin around and spring to life
and the street signs turn violently
the squares of every large city
turn people around madly
they turn back out of fear
they turn back with hope or even without hope
In any event, in the midst of squares
it isn't easy to stand still
the turning of others grabs and carries you off
since at Omonia
every passer-by
every machine
whether they like it or not
must move in circles
no one is interested in learning
the reason for all this turning
they are confined to the dizziness of others
and, such is life, today the people
kill all the cacophony inside them
in the dizziness of circles.

Harbour

The sky has melted and the bodies and hearts sweat
the stone is burning from the smashing of hopes
gone to live in the harbour joints
with wine and women and lads and hashish
the sun scorches the earth from which desires climb
seagulls flying below funnels and sails on the spray of toil
melted from the weight of the many ships.

In the harbour ships sleep side by side
the blows of well-trained hammers lull them to sleep
– caressing the iron with unyielding words –
the steel speaks – reciting its powerful story with an echo
the workers print it with their tired hands
and the passer-by hears it reverberating in the sheds
while watching underneath the shovels
the coal, the soil of Santorini, the limestone regurgitate
the whisper of the broken bodies of stevedores.

They burn up slowly slowly from the summer sun
from their fire the harbour is lit up with the colour of labour
barrels, coal, boxes, sacks, wood, wheat, bricks, sand
in holds, in barges, inside wagons
everywhere the shadows emerge of workers hammering the harbour
entwining the coal with the earth, the steel with water
money with wealth, work with slavery
and their broken backs with grave tuberculosis.

All day long the effort strains the endurance
the hammering of a day's work has a hollow sound to the poor
cheap is the noise of a bent backbone
only uncouth money shimmers – its masses dazzle both eyes
and the willpower which kneel lay down in dire poverty
heavy the weight of this place – the tone of the stevedore
on its scales it remains insensitive to words of compassion
the folded fingers alone push the weights

but the barges the red and the black
lasciviously swell the waters of the harbour
drink the workers' bodies – keep them –
going back and forth – with sacks and shovels
today white – yesterday black
and their silent story is carried by a foul rhapsody
from mouth to mouth
to the beat of the stevedores' paces
one of them throws in a couple of words
with the coal, the other one catches them
and so the story goes from morning till noon
the next day begins in a similar way
now and then a cigarette breaks it
the purchased water sells it with new words
that is all
but it is a great deal
to the iron fences of the stevedores.

The grey, the black ships
the grey, the red warehouses
all of it – the horizon of a day
ugly in its monotony
from the images the sun
illuminates spitting its heat
the green terrains of the sea swallow the oil
and the waterfalls of the mountain are photographed in the ships' vomit
the watermelon rinds walk in gardens amongst the barges
where the children of Atlas reign
lifting the insides of the earth onto their bare backs
the stevedores.
Soon though this will also be taken from them
the teeth, the claws of the cranes
will let the horrifying grimace of coal
dragging the wounds of the faces
wash itself through unemployment.

Erotic

When the sky spreads out the shadows of cities
the illuminated spheres of the streets burn with unappeasable joy
swirling their gaze around erotically distorting everything they see
lights then rip up the created nature, voices thrown onto the streets
from the sides of houses or the dark side streets
lights are tossed from those who stand in the corners
and eyes of petrol-driven joy make the concrete dizzy
while lithe bodies seductively light up the night
rubbing sensually the twin rails with their swift passage
around there in the Klaxon voices singing from lifeless branches
indiscreet lamps lay bare the darkness
for ablaze or half-dead flesh to roll
in seductive straight lines of insatiable desires
on the concrete
thirsty backbone which trembles
only with the heavy tread of vans
the wide avenues saturated with the sperm of oil
moist their lips for passing bodies to luxuriate
in the ceaseless slither
the slither on the stretched out earth
the cars slither, the engines slither
running insatiably, furiously, sensually
through the squares
through the remote endless and entangled streets
of big cities
cities expanded by the night
nothing can hide anymore in their strange life
the rich lights register everything and all that they forget
shadows of fantastic houses or the imprints of lifeless things are added
by showing sensual fragments that emerge from doors, windows, corners
vampires struck dumb by the sound of metallic voices
now adorning the residential streets
their voices and words alone matter
and they are harsh heavy

painful are the kisses of iron
that copulate with the tremor of engines
with the jolt of motors
the melodic stopping of the brake hurts
when it is dragged along the unripe end of a sudden turn
and in the midst of the noise it is difficult to hear
the wooden heel of a female licking the cobblestone
sensations even crazier light up the cities now
every night, every moment of the night
the chase of motors heats up life
cars limousines big small buses and trams
turn the streets erotically
crossing trucks pedestrians
going up, coming down with joy and pleasure
falling, tumbling down, being torn apart with erotic mania
inside cities, dizzy from mad flashes the night forgets herself
shamelessly putting into motion her secret wheels
which turn unbelievably fast bestowing nations
with beauty more profound than mountains with running waters
harmonies more breath-taking than the erotic calls of sweet-singing birds
today the machines are in gigantic cities where they germinated much more than just foolish kids
they are not just a soul
but a thing
soft grass where erotic games blossom
the machines are in cities tyrannized by seducing attractions
sensuous fruit for the people in multi-storeyed houses
granted their blood something like the fragrance of petroleum
that which blurs the dreams
with a sweet peculiar blue haze
often driving bleeding efforts to accidents
where necrophilic steering-wheels debauch
but there are no convictions for these crimes
nor will the murders decrease
with hysterical nostalgia for the old ways of life
or with the threats of rusted hands
and the barren blasphemies spilling

the shabby bodies of this rust
love is indifferent to pain and breaking and goes on
sadistically injuring beings
then swallowed up by roads scattered with engines
for the creative convulsion of propellers and wheels to flare up.

Santorini

I

In moments of fire I believed
that the sweet mauve casting a shadow on the island's waters
opens up unassailable depths
mirrors of hope, of eyes, of pleasures
and I was glad

from the top of those mountains that break the dark blue
    harmony I believed
that in the craters of vertigo futile expressions burn
children of books, of knowledge and laws
and I was glad

I believed this when I saw the caiques embracing the winds
but now when I see them in the sleep of morning tied to the pier
I only see the hard frames of their sails
and dead now to each gust
I look out at the horizons of the archipelago
I am a simple caique owner
in a harbour of unseen depths.

II

Black and tall are the mountains of my island
taller still since the red of her earth is as deep and black as the bottom
    of the sea
turbid from its walks on the horizon together with the winds
now when the boats have set sail for other seas
the surrounding wilderness floods with memories caressing the cliffs
where time passed lightly lightly, when the nights were painted azure
but the blue eyes have been lost, since they went away the sea is silent
and I like to think that their colour faded in the foams of a
    foreign land

their untravelled journey might not have pained the earth
neither deepened the waves nor disturbed the sea beds
insignificant, some change to these lands arrived by a gust of
 desolation
from that day when the mating game of escape stained them with
 waiting

III

The sea was unexpectedly cut into by a cruel ship
and the water incessantly softens the precipitous shape of the cliffs
brusque words and acts of life chiselled the summit
prepared by nature for greater beauty
but all of this is bound together by an inexplicable harmony
and sometimes in hours plump with the heat of noon or on
 heavy nights
it presses down on dry lips thirsty for the power of silent moments
– drops unknown to minds cultivated at the piers of Venetian
 islands –
what does it matter though which desires grow in the Cycladic life
since the Aegean hammers out the shapes illuminating its surface
– perfect diversion to the eye seasoned by the secrets of beauty.

That is for the other, poor spectators of the waves –
As if they don't know that the sea bed remains quiet from such
 heavy weight.

IV

With a scream in the night the lighthouse frightens the tall cliffs
and makes them play gigantic games
spreading their revels from the sky to the polyphonic caves
for hours the immense screams of desperate shadows sound
 from faraway
heroic words alone can break this material into rhythms
but the pleasures that Santorini offers a person

quickly transform the passions, breaking every Cyclopean gust
upon the porcelain of the mountains that whitewash her black beauty.
From there the island gazes theatrically at the volcano that created her
and watches its workings with the perfection of bewitching supremacy.
Drunk now from so many contradictory fluids
I bow down, and unwittingly for a moment become the
   spectator of the play in which I perform.

Only beauty remains and underlines our difference.

V

The harshest of the Cycladic islands has now been given away
   to other horizons
and my night was rigged with the sails of drunken remembrance
but strong is the hurling of the winds hauling our thoughts to and fro
and if the ground I now walk on sweetly smells of fat flowers
I give these lascivious scents to lips either more or less lustful
my body thirsts for yellow smoke and soil of fire
gardens with many blossoms, tulips, jasmines, broad-leafed roses
I leave them to hands weaving maiden garlands or crowns of
   necrophilia.
Leave me to imagine those heads that I love encircled
by the fruits granting me the juices for my overflowing glass.
I want no cluttered gardens, no dizziness of winter flowers
I am frightened by the Hymettus mountain's tremor of spring beneath
   the shadow of daffodils
I yearn for the waste land, the wild, the red earth that educates
with fire and smoke and thunder, with what pain life is built.

VI

On the crumbling cliffs, the remnants of Oia strip the earth
and when they speak you can still hear them dream of
    Ptolemaic triremes.
Dragging their heavy load from the Sea of Crete
to the black shores surrounding dangerous Santorini.
I want her to be the reason instead of some more Christian
forcing the temple of Isis with no worshippers to look at the sun
to light up the sea, the rocks and to evaporate the water.
On its wet surface the shadows once showed the sails the way
    that leads to the Nile.
Without a purpose the palaces now see the centuries smile to
    other rhythms
without spectators the ancient theatre of Oia
is showing a drama recited by the winds when wild Thera is furious
so as to upset all who might enjoy a peaceful sleep.

VII

The long summer nights have died
and the dappled shadows of autumn now illuminate other glories
and joys, misty from the flood of memory's rainfall.
The memories have now drowned the island travels with their
    downpours
it's gone, it's all over, the desires that gave birth to them gone
    up in smoke
the waves caressing those pleasures have dried up
sea-shells, pebbles, their garrulous game on the coast of waiting
    have come to a halt
the cruel shores deserted they see the north wind hauling the clouds
in the sky that I loved for the sweet song of its falling stars.
They've gone, the long summer nights have died
and the deep autumn shadows flicker out the suns
light up unknown lives of mine and warm up with their weak rays
silent breathless craters, extinct craters.

VIII

Santorini, an arid word to me now
ashes in my memory
born out of a ship fire that banished me from rugged shores
to blur my desires, my dreams, with the soaring smoke of cities.
This is where I live now – on flatlands swelling with houses
clenching its hearts within walls, on streets.
Thera's heavy masses of rocks leisurely spread the hopes on
    her naked slopes.

Often for no reason during the day, or at night I am overtaken
    by spells
which unsettle my existence with the dangers of that island.
the sea bed still quakes and its turmoil perverts the colour of the
    Aegean's salty waters.

And yet, for the destruction of the harmonious continuation of
    its azure appearance
the violent movements of the winds sufficed – the rain
sufficed – superfluous this obtrusive interruption
of profound disquiet to the precarious surface of so many troubles.

Columns of the Temple of Olympian Zeus

At night the azure columns of the temple turned pale
but in vain lift their wounded stature to unreachable skies
no one understands the silent prayer of old worship
which through the evocative lines of chiselled stone led to Zeus
the acanthus ornaments have rusted and the fearless capitals are
    windblown all over
by erotic breaths taking shelter over here
the marbles have been reduced to being liturgists of Hymen
they have lost all other meaning
archaeologists try in vain to find any coherence
in fragments that history has thrown far away
the silenced fragments lie on the ground
disturbed no more by the footsteps of the faithful
no shadow resounds through the ruins
that also betrayed my walk
its purpose lost in the distant roof of the starless night
and the coherence of my history is lost, never again to be found.

I envied the cold slabs of stone
silently standing here for centuries now
listening to the sweet echo of past emotions.

Minoan

I

In the realms of people now dead for thousands of years
I remembered the cruel perfection of her beauty
Phaistos Knossos are the names of places that enchanted me.
These ruins steer a powerful imagination
to perfections no less cruel.

Calamities, raids, new glories
seemed unable to completely erase
that which so skilfully had originally been engraved.

II

From Minoan times the beautiful girl at the Cretan museum.

Will you ever have the fate of being worshipped in an enclosed room
  by wise men coming from all over the world after three thousand
  years?
Yet your beauty is today unequalled.
Today.

These concerns are for you – crafter of your own beauty –
it is the price of your transient supremacy
and these words of mine like ancient coins
used in payment by all those who know how to value what they see.

III

What was Phaistos like in the glory days?
My admiration was above all for Phaistos.
Was the palace even more imposing?
And you in a few years' time without the exquisite picture of your face
what will you be like?

Superficial the supremacy of art
its ruins fail to differ sufficiently from its work.

IV

Without a landing place the stairs of the palace carries footsteps up
showing an enchanting view underlined by ruins:
mountains, fields – remnants of an old civilization
Beauty – Art.

In the past this magnificent staircase had more use,
its purpose now gone
and our efforts in essence have an empty echo.
Eleven pine-trees only – I counted them –
hold out – for hours now the wind is blowing –
singing of this death.

V

There are no vast palaces here
imposing staircases – grand entrances
no regal chambers to dazzle your eyes
and the ruins are poor
the homes of ordinary people – workers.
They must have suffered
their houses burnt down.
But similar to now the lives then
rolled by in silent pain.

And so also their ruins –
very meagre to the mattock of the archaeologist
not even the name of the place has survived.
The Minoan slaves have no history.

And if they had, why should it be written down?

VI

Admired by wise men
the rich civilization of Ancient Crete.
– Not just wealth – unequalled art
which is also hygienic.
Cleanliness being unknown in the days of Pericles
– glorious aqueducts long before Eupalinos –
in Phaistos at Knossos.

From Gournia is discernible
an island from where lepers are hurled.

VII

And the Grecian is beautiful:
this ancient relief
flawless portrait of an adolescent boy.

One night I saw –
the same model playing in a high mountain village of Crete.

If I were a sculptor –
and successfully chiselled the marble there would be no point.

Poverty and Art
forever doomed to discover new ways of expression.

VIII

'This is where the Middle Minoan wall begins
over there – to your right – it is covered by the foundations of Late
    Minoan buildings.'
That is more or less what my guide told me.
Cheap words.
The work renders the tool useless – the mattock.
The archaeologist in particular a turner of shapes
and the art of creating ruins
true poetry
lines – interruptions of lines
unattainable example of artistic simplicity.

IX

At least
since Crete was destroyed and the Mycenae
if only the invaders had fallen silent
– they were barbarians
and the art of the Aegean too much for them.
But they kept talking.

It could be worse though
And to this day Phidias' works of art are salvaged.

Notebooks
(1933–1936)

Revolution

The entire world of the eye, the entire world – crosses
and the world of other eyes crosses as well
from within the earth the dead warm bodies of soldiers.
From the earth crosses shoot up
crosses on graves at weddings and crosses before and after.
And in the two wreaths lemon blossoms now unwithering blossoms
for the veiled brides of the crosses.
Tightly, tightly, their snow-white veils painted black
– upon the same bodies, the insatiable body of the bride
hurled to the ground, the erotic call of their tears
and in other beds, the other weddings.
The kisses of a sister for her brother and of a daughter on her
 father's cross
the tragic wedding, the kisses of a mother for her son
the other weddings, brother with brother
the wailing of the veils, the call of the night
the black sheets of a night's orgies, the secret erotic kisses
the kissing of the dead and the crosses, the entire world of the eye –
 crosses
the earth the sky and up there the angels dressed in moonlight
half-moons and angels and songs
as in heaven so on earth, and the stars descend
and the half-moons move rhythmically
each of them above its familiar cross
cutting the cross as if it was the ear of corn, oh, if only it was corn
and the black dry wood was weighed down with straw
and the women's eyes were flowers of the field
and the women's weeping was bird song
and their prayers were kisses
and the kisses were feast-days for children, oh what joy
my heart is beating, it is beating like a hammer.

I would like to make my own sky
so that I would have a firmament to look at now when night has
 fallen

I would make it big, full of stars with strange shapes
instead of just one, I would place two different moons there
one small as a child, the other big as grievance.
The two of them would not always follow each other
the first would go to sleep up north
and the big one would pass over my clock to chime midnight.
At times when they would walk side by side
like a pair of blue eyes – the eyes of blindness
they would see all which fear has created
they would see tossed away close to me
words – the words from the day
and the moons would chase me
and their moonshine would nail me down
and one would quietly speak the language of regret
and the other would passionately run through the firmament
in new orbits
and so the new order of the two-mooned sky
would look like madness
and my eyelids would close and open from the incense of their
 harmony.
A double game of circles now covers the sky
melodies in pairs heard by my ears for the first time
born by the invisible chords of the moons
eternal motifs for mandolins and serenades
and while the numbers of moons increase –
a full wreath of white balls the sky
bright wheels roll and rise
and lift up the sky.
Before sunrise kisses can be heard
it is the sound of the moons falling and getting hurt.
When I wake up, I wake up from fatigue my body looks as if it
 has suffered.

And the green fell into the blue
and it turned grey that eye
a light grey
a simple shadow across the expression
it turned the eye everywhere – left and right, up and down

now that it has been set free from its unbearable body
a planet big and bright
star for the steps of a miracle-worker
– but the miracle-workers have died
and I drag my feet in their aimless walk
in the city on the mountains on the coast
to my inhospitable naked bed
and the eye wanders like a sphere in chaos
like a brilliant sun – which sweet light, the slight light of the moon –
like a burning sun, that you gaze upon, that you cannot see
like a sun like a divine eye
the eye of love
endows sleep with sleeplessness
and my dream with nightmares
dawn remodels its colour before erasing it
like the caress a beautiful opal in the sunbeams
turning it blue
with some rose-coloured lines reminiscent of coral
afterwards that emerald green prevails
which wanders in dewy grass
the green comes after the unbearable yellow traces of a weary life.

When I wake up – I wake up feeling tired
the eye wide open still watches me
playing with the colours painted by so many loves
playing with the colours unfolding the furrows of the other eyes
the beloved eyes of foreign bodies
eyes full of hope
and were closed shut so as not to see but they saw
eyes that loved
and now they no longer know which is preferable
to stay open or shut.

Athens 1933

Now that the children of other bourgeois trample upon the
 silence of the orators, the sophists
Teutons – fallen patricians, heroes of many deaths in Venice –
English poets with Wildean forms and Byronic scandals,
Egyptian and foreign victories are carried to her arenas and
 sporting fields,
and regular patrons of her life gave birth to those children of the
 Greek nation
who, from countries where Maximus of Ephesus worked wonders,
from lands of other faiths
every day, on ships of bankrupt firms, arrive at Athens...
it is time for us to abandon the grounds of her collapsed walls.
Alone now in the evenings of the summer months let her watch
the sun hiding behind the rusted columns
while for the last time she plays with the watery images of Ilisos.
They have been constructed to water the ends of the earth with
 the glory of a city that washes itself in a waterless river
with whatever remains from this glory.
And there is no hope for their constitution to change
for the river bed to be covered with more water.
For the Athenians to drown they must now look elsewhere for
 their sepulchral bath.

Narcissus 1934

Now when hope is directed towards the past
when the hour of decisions no longer shall return
the sea-ways the timbered roadways are setting on other horizons
it is to his own body that he returns
on the expanse of stagnant waters he keeps watch for
the image of a wrinkled shrivelled up and repulsive Narcissus
the image that Narcissus did not wish to give him.

Pre-Myth

I continue:
Poetic decree, I name the stages of my liberation efforts
Notebooks. I summon the Tenth and Torch-bearing Muse! Let sparks of her will grace my verse with movement! They will not be lost! This is the command of our times, that nothing will be lost! How fiery the intensity, the passion in thought! Almost nothing is visible, but each practice has its appointed place. Thus only the new changes the old. Our criterion is the criterion of history: the destination of man. Laws of contracts and claims to ownership – more specifically, closer to poetry – intellectual ownership, are all in its service. The appropriation of verses, foreign or our own, is often enforced. Only Pharisees can escape from themselves and others, they falsify! Good poems are those that bring results. Cowards are afraid of results, they are anti-poetic characters. But art is a powder-keg, proof: the Parthenon!

In darkness, carrying the weight of all that has been, we move with Herculean force to secure the timeliness of our objectives. The effort must be continued all through our existence! When continuity is interrupted time is reincarnated, the future changes residence. Look at the statues of Mesopotamia, the Cyclades, of Easter Island and the Tang Dynasty! Daedalus leaves Ionia and turns into Brancusi. The perpetual light of Vermeer van Delft awakens Salvador Dali – towards which point on the frightening horizon of his landscapes are we moving? – I ask Heraclitus, Pythagoras, Empedocles, the great Ions of modern times, Hegel, Richter, von Kleist, and the other German Romantics, their French brothers, Nerval, Lautréamont, Rimbaud, the Anglo-Saxons Donne, Blake and Poe. Sounds also advance; their forgotten beginning carries us to oriental love songs, to jazz, to *Madame Butterfly*, to *Bolero*. A day will come when some Tino Rossi will sing a sonnet by Shakespeare. The horizon of the phonograph already surpasses the boundaries of earth.

Let the frenzy be continued, the super heroic course is always far away from the end and the beginning without ever losing its reason and purpose therewith. Let the spark become a flame! So many who loved her betray her through worship. There is an oncoming plague of sceptics and Pharisees!

Without falsification, with love and hate towards the private parts, we are transporting our very BEING at full speed in time!

Let not this blasphemy be heard again: 'Prometheus has grown tired!' Sleep was made to serve man, its purpose is LIFE. We are not alone and we are not just spectators and the spectators are not always spectators!

It traverses space, the

LET THERE BE FIRE

Contract with Demons

The hopes returned   their untrodden path
and what was lost has been named light
all that has happened returns together with what will become
when I arrive again where I now am
I will be able to walk in darkness as well as alone and in silence.

Unforgettable love returns again
it brought memory and hope to the desires
and offered with words of your unconscious plea
my will to emerge from criminal listlessness
to emerge and to gush forth with elation that great gift
and without hesitation the sun-drenched decision of so so many.

I cannot live unless another past is found for me
I have reached the first years of my existence
see how it piles up struggles and extends my dreams beyond the night
they cover all of my efforts   I am left alone
I have reached the first years of my existence
I would like not to turn ahead   the days about to come they know me well
  how can they hold any secrets since I do not forget?
It is not here   it was the dream of a dream now lost between inhaling and exhaling
neither I nor my desire held out against the horror
the hopes still fight the yearnings   a repugnant kiss escapes my body
it was early unimaginably early for each patience
all which is given to our heart by memory thus fails to lose its freshness
all of the interest that engages us dries us up as well.

Torchbearing desires walk ahead
while the same number of lamps mingle with shadows of the past
in the light an invisible end blinds an indeterminate figure
iridescent love and intellect   fear encloses its purple robe
the scent of aromatic oils and incense falls on its head as the single ornament
and the gaze looks intently only at things to come.

No one will come or has ever come to him   this is no reason
    for us not to wait
each day increases the space separating the similar from the
    dissimilar
no hope   shadows everywhere pain and desires and the
    remains of faith that return again.

The past was born today   of a sort   it is mine
it will come it will fall on top of us   nor does it stay back when
    I fall behind
every swiftness seems futile nothing else exists
shapes left unchangeable by flesh become important
I begin to play some role in my own existence
I follow the past that goes ahead of me.

Neither words nor hopes count
a yearning begins   bringing its commands
it does not tell us where it comes from or where it is going maybe
    we will never see it
I follow it   I mimic you   it is enough it allows me to forget
    and to endure
the obstacles that appear I believe they were raised for me
I struggle to bring them down   thus some coherence is found in
    so many contradictions
a stranger to words to acts and to hopes   fallen into deep oblivion.

What do we want with the light that covers us?
the extensions of time from all around us
the things that matter that only we understand without
    understanding them very well
they free us from doubts and pettiness
we rise at the invitation call without a clear idea of what direction we
    are heading
the things that matter resound at the bottom of our hearts they
    disturb and upset

we are unsettled.
Neither retribution nor remorse is enough
the one is forbidden the other shatters rhythms
better all beloved to become a flame
and my own semen pain poison
between the legs and their loathsome bed
and whatever our destiny come what may
the time has come for pleasure to rule again
the new idol of whole nights from surmise day dream
reaches fulfilment   brings me there
from opportunity cause becoming a hymn
trumpets sound unforeseen victory
beauty ceases to comprise the anticipation of memories
desires gaze upon pleasure and if I am left alone again
whatever is mine watches and will see
in doubts the flashes of an unknown certainty in decay
the disembodied reins of relations unforeseen directions of
    reciprocity
they are not insignificant
our bodies were in a state of readiness forever suspending their
    own offering.

They bring us ungovernable passions we abandon ourselves
    nothing goes away
moments that never happened take place in the past
without a will or a desire for will I toss about I talk I goad on I believe
I now struggle against the words
a thousand dreams call out the sea the sea and death death
a gipsy woman is leafing through the hours   devoutly I kiss her hands.

I am waiting for a day to break without ruins or worries
a dawn where everything will be as I wished it to be
for joy to stretch into the sea into your eyes
to reach the fingertips
an error a colossal mistake are the roads already travelled to me
I wish to find the traces of shadows proof of isolation and
    exquisite moments where there is no isolation.

Like damnation like conscience like an enemy armed to the teeth
    and always visible it comes
like the Jews like Sappho like Salome like all the persecuted
we get a glimpse of the smoke still rising during this century

I call out to you in the middle of the night
the speed of the voice is lost in the void
what will happen to you where will I go?

If only I could surrender to pain without suffering
to become grief and yours and lust
I would gladly give you expanses to be transformed by your heart
    into wounds
what pleasure for nights where I shall be alone
and for the other nights with no dreams.

The hopes were dismembered   a cry escapes the void
drowning in the wave   silence showed itself in all its magnitude
I have no luck   they named her Kallisti – the most beautiful
vision apparition illusion memory all now belongs to oblivion
In that case new pains will be laid to my memory
I shall cross oceans of fire
far beyond the recollections
to the anticipations of untouched lips
to the beaches of a grey islet
the image reaches beyond August
it reaches the deeds of the past and the future
all is lost both sorrows and indifference
I implore and savour the desire
belated feelings are transformed into reminiscences
knowledges and talents to be exact I add to the pleasures
guide to all that I was and I stumble and fall and fail to recognize.

The sun set the hand of my Mistress it withdrew
and when she was about to die
no one hated as much as I did
I pass through dawn   at the hour of Kallisti!

Paris–Athens–Santorini, 1934–1935–1936

When the Eyes Last No Longer

Night has sealed the lips, night has fallen everywhere, without love sorrow plays
The dream and the sea have no beginning and the distance is not suspended, the horizon never ceases to deceive us
As the violins play, clocks and skeletons invite the singers of funeral laments to bring down the clouds
Crowds open up and appear with faces warm and smooth
Their voices faint, doctors and hangmen and magi have eliminated the harmony of their chords
They were locked up, all those memories bringing moonbeams, green drops and melodies of the sand and the wind
The spring water no longer descends, and the pleasure remains, blood stops the desires of false sensibilities, the all-white body shudders, all around anemones await
Whereto the lit up road, why the abduction, the scattered feelings, the kiss with nothing but love and dust?
The heart is like a cave, heartlessly spreading and vanishing
Everything is like a heart
Listen to what they are saying in the corridors, how the pulse is beating, the rain is falling, the people retreating, listen to the silence and fill it!
Fill it with decisive winds, the winds with wishes, the wishes with pain, the pain with skin unimaginably sweet to the touch of your own body, with shivers and warmth, with pictures with words with shame desire and lust, with twenty autumns and no spring at all.
Listen to what will happen: the news spread over the mountains, cross the streets, disturb the waters, colour the light, open the graves, burn the crops, aromatize everything

Unprecedented colours will fill the paintings, the
 pleasures of the eye will have no end, the pain will
 feed on never-ending surprises, old age will be
 punished and youth eternally eternal
 For eternities of eternities

1937

The
French
Poems
(1937–1940)

To Travel out of the Past

Reclaim the day
Give it the image and the surprised dream
Love is split in two
Let us return forward toward the radiance of new faces
And the words which carry efficacious gestures far beyond all commands

Let us fix with a new precision the dramatic movement
Of ships with no prow or sail
Conquered or conqueror to be fixed in flaming love

I need your tears and to be unjust!

The day is no more than the chance appearance of your eyes
Monstrous hour without great acts of shattering remembrance
Like that self of myself that another has seen
I was given
A stranger to my shadow he stays chained to my footsteps
Like the moon mother-of-pearl to the tide
And the veil to mourning
When the waiting is over
The light will rise to your eyes
As I am you will never see me again not even in words
When fate shows its most wicked cards

The rest is atrocious!

Conquered or conqueror by a love put to death
Torn apart
By the water the blood the thousand splinters of broken voices
The painful violence that has taken hold of our hands
Will spray the hair with serpents
And all the ink of the words thrown behind

Athens 1937–Lisbon 1940

The Agony in the Crowd

To die unwrinkled by the breath of fire
To hate death
To pursue madness further beyond the dream
Water, air and all sciences
To respond to them all

Listen to the noise of men retreating
Hangmen, magi, doctors
Nothing horrifies them
Anguish is without mercy
Tomorrow's moon has already become their closest caress
They are like blind men imprisoned by distance

At the summit of tranquillity
I AM
I rest
Like the man drowned in his misfortune

Athens 1937–Marrakesh 1938

The Ruins of a City

Let us make dawn the subject of a crime
At noon let us invent stars on the horizon of a journey
Stars and a new ornament for hours with no tomorrow
Disembowelled ships raise anchor
Their blood is heavy with rust
Everything swims in vermin
A cat that can no longer cry eats them
From the top of the Tower of the Winds flames rise up
And drown the light
The tower is tall ablaze and has broken loose from Earth
The Earth!
Who condemned it to live like a peeled orange
Or a blue grain of sand
Subject to the perpetual yoke of two equinoxes?
The insistent rhythm
The hideous expectation of eclipses is there
Wherever we go

Athens 1937–Marrakesh 1939

The Massacre of Innocent

The night of a rupture
The irrefutable testimony
A heart long traumatized
Blood no longer distinguished from semen
Nor words from urine
Between shame and hope
By starting again this time with shame
I was alone in my love for asphodels
And the screams of their withered stems
What ship
How many years of horror?
In the land of minuscule mummified heads
We could wear for a tie
Our worst enemy
But I have no enemy to replace my tie
And the dog I loved was not mine
The ships have lost their masts
The checks bounced
The murderer has no crime
I can no longer distinguish the faces of passers-by
And the past without images
When you find a mandrake
All had not yet been stolen or devoured
Blood and words flowed freely

Athens 1937–Lisbon 1940

In a Time Still Unfinished

The lip is still red
The hand deformed by waiting
Maintain the effort and expect the obstacles
Chance pursues oblivion

His body is without reflexes
His breath is made of the most beautiful memory
His kiss is silence

The silence is broken

The curve of the head ends in a cross
Bad luck weighs on us and on its dark head
Glory turns to bitterness
Gold to rust
Desires and sorrows together lift the wind

The lover of the chiromancer is a vigilant lover
His face is covered in blood
His transparent eyes pierced by water
He brandishes the nightmares

She emerges from the red and green sea like an object of hope

Gigantic experimenter
Makes the blood gush from the scars
Rectify the heart of love mangled
Rectify the work of false prophets
For you everything is Ardour and Game
In the infernal fear of violent ruptures

Athens 1937–Paris 1939

Song of Oblivion

Fill the silence!
We need the wind of clamour of wishes of torrents of pain
Naked daggers their golden reflection
Hardened fears of delirious ships
Make the iron blades sing
Shed drops of fire into your tears
Merge flames with your hair
Snakes with your footsteps
The echo of the mountains with your voice
The waves with your dreams
Madness with mirrors
We need monsters to fill the crevasses
And all the seduction of the sources
All the anger of the oppressed!

When love is nothing but vertigo
The night the embrace of a dream
Childhood a cruel game
Rivers of blood will soak the deserts
Swept away by fast horses and sails mated with assault tanks that coil around themselves
Let us merge the hoarse voice of the cloth merchant
The depressing virtue of girls
With the sound of abandoned bells!

We will overtake the wind and the night
Leaving behind us the shrill music of strings atrociously taut
And the stifled screams beneath the masks
The mountains advance under a thunderstorm of drums
Close the orifices of the cities
Arrest the blind the lepers the jealous
Nail the beggars to the door of tyrants
Release the clairvoyants
Cover the sky in poems
Terrify the world!

When everything is happening
The levy in mass
The divorce
The short-circuit
Canker
Nothing can stop the news
It uproots the shade from trees
Snatches the ink from printing presses
And all memories
It coagulates the blood and the sea
Bends the iron
Firms the sand
Merges urine with fire
And makes sperm a new look of hate

Full of hope
From the rooftops cats play with the stars
From the trees toads sing a new hosanna

The world is once again full of promises and delirious objects
This week the surprises are endless
And victorious shocks are on show
Let us borrow centuries of infinity
Poems with wheels of fire have arrived
The triangles are spinning like wheels
The violins are like swords
Youth is Defiance Space and Violence
It is FIRE
Our enemies are condemned in advance to build immense pyramids

Always higher
Never high enough to rise above the level of a raging sea
Tormented upset fed by all our passions
Our enemies are victorious
But in their defeat transparent water and with no reflection
Will cover their sordid bodies
Heavy water fused with sleep without dreams

Athens 1937–Meknes 1939

The Dance of the Survivors

Let us create destiny
Remind the infinite of the rhythm of audacity
Reconnect support to instinct and life to life
The clock with no hands in a lighthouse with no lights
The ship navigates between slow passages
The thought has fallen
Everything turns purple and becomes a ritual
Destiny is free rapid violent
Everything reaches immense proportions
The wall creaks slowly then collapses
Destiny is made up of infinitely small and terribly scattered elements
Everything becomes immense immense an immense bread roll
And is headed towards this window that overlooks the madness
And a tiny little yard where the vermin is swarming
All dancing stops then starts again
Around the window where the vermin sing

Athens 1937–Paris 1938

The Blue of the Dream

What to do with these shreds of badly fused images?
The cities of remembrance await the wind of the ruins
In your hands the walls have shattered
The dream rises to the surface
Caress the flames with your eyes!
Inhale their perfume!
Let us play with the irreplaceable
Oblivion can expand everything
For you all is grand
Ruin's dice respond to my call
And make shadow the tide of a lifetime
Relentless returns are breaking the waves
All the sand of the earth would no longer be enough to cover the eyes with sleep
The fearful succession of dreams would no longer be enough to populate my night
What dream what obscenity what regret could save us?
If hope frightens you, give it to me!
If my words frighten you, let us spread out the silence!
If my presence frightens you, let us shatter the vastness!
Oblivion escaped to the back of a mirror
And drinks the dew of your forehead
It lives in the future and in everything you have left behind
The anguish of the past defies the worst nightmares
Your silence
The desert where I advance
The vertigo of return
Render immobile the slightest events of the day
Already a name surprised in the unknown thinks like a bad memory

Paris 1938–New York 1940

The Storm at Dawn

The heart of a child is in flames
Open to him the road of tears when in the night his shadow comes undone
Without a reflection in his hand without a mirror to be sure of himself
He wakens his grief tears it out and then eats it

Escaped from a dream the moon has dropped from his hands
The water remains impassive darkens only slightly cools
The town fades hunting cars emptying the houses uprooting the trees
And sheds his blood into the river
Some will be spared
Spiders will lose their web
Heroes their glory
The sky is blue with pain
Anguish has eyes that will never close again
At crossroads the red lights remain on
Only chance advances
Its blaze intense and monstrous devours the flames

Paris 1938

The Great Misunderstood

Waiting in a wave
The audacity around us
Rain and venom
All are elements of this turbulent return

Come back like a folded pocket knife
An umbrella closed again
The heart full of disgust

It has invaded everything
Despite the night the broken disc breaks through the door
And everything we have ever stolen
Time to rest or to escape
Nothing responds
Where to discover the sacrifices?
I want to become the oracle of my life
The horizon is but a breath without a face
A monster sitting in the sand among torn newspapers
And these rare objects intended for someone who remains unknown
To all it opposes this force which spreads sorrow, shame and rapid departures
This force that gives numbers and days an evil meaning

Paris 1938

Oedipus is Innocent

Tomorrow there will be nothing left
The skin on our hands will again become dust
In spring there will be no stars
Resinous blood will flow in our veins
The earth will be opened like those doors which we will never
    again close
The whole earth will be like a wound all year round
We will no longer need a compass
There will be no future no audacity no stars
No one will pass
No head as tall as having to bend down
Gestures will have no meaning
All sides of the dice will be the same
The desert like glaciers

O hair happy island of a mirage!

I have no more secrets from anyone
I killed it all
All that was violently cherished and deposited in my life
Swept away by the current I sleep in a liquid bed
A sleep full of noises
In an endless night

Paris 1938–Meknes 1939

Narcissus in the Desert

Three faces in a single one
Too much sand for the sun
Give fire to madness
Its liquid shadow spreads out

A new rupture is on the horizon

The mirror is too sharp
From its touch the eyes die of thirst
And look aside
The paper remains white and neutral and dry as space
Solder the support to life
Follow the trail
Make a poem violent as a mirage
Drink with love these three faces in one
Flood your hair
And Narcissus will have lived

Meknes 1939

Torn from Mirrors

In falling the dream is broken
I found oblivion in a drowned mirror
Intoxicated with anxiety
Devoured by fear
I drank from that water which no light has ever caressed
As an object leans over its shadow
I now see love under an oblique ray
Who makes me bend my head?
Upsets the hour?
How to reach again the sun without breaking through dawn?
Detach fear from all images and I will swim in the vastness of oblivion!
By the same gesture
Getting lost and finding the direction of things
Beyond left and right
Beyond audacity and the horizon
Beyond the wind

The wind of fear
A ghastly wind almost immutable
That tears out the echo buried in sand
And the smoke imprisoned in fossils
That steals from jackals their dreams
From infants their future
A wind which in its embrace betrays its rage

Plunged into distress I drowned my star

In this rectilinear fall a new face appears
The light devours it
And opposes to chance all that remains of me
In the inevitable rhythm of disaster
I could say before the end of the day
All the mirrors are thirsty
One stroke of an oar suffices to drown a star
Without reflections without shadows the heart slowly dies
And makes memory a perpetual sleeplessness

Avenger and conqueror of myself
I swear by these thrusts of destiny
A ferocious world of violent ideas will arise
Its image engraved in the most lucid eye
Already defies the capricious temper of the prophets
Spikes the mirrors
Raises the bloodied heads of black bulls

Paris 1939–Lisbon 1940

Starless Departure

Like the memory of water underneath the ship and the hour of
    the greatest secrets
Your name is blue like the blue of a flame and of hope
I wanted to crush it
To stain your warm blood and drown my audacity
Blood was lost in the laments
I have lost the key to your dreams
I have lost you like a penny repeated a million times
I was jealous of myself
And the vastness of the seas

But it is you I pity
Your travels without dreams
Your parched nights
Your hair playing with itself
Your dreams without mirrors cold like the desire of another
Traces of blood light up the face

I am infinitely more than the rich and voluptuous colour of a crime
More than a mirror for your eyes
More than your departure
More than an uncertain future
I walk without an echo
Your return would add nothing
Together we are too many for ourselves
Too much like a defeated army or a poor harvest
Everything smells of betrayal a dream interrupted a thought
    escaping the wind
The waiting for a blind-born
Before I knew you the fire was sacred
Now it is Earth that has come crashing down
We will invent something else
A heart that runs like an infernal machine
A sinusoid or a new kite
A new space a new colour for the dawn

Not everything has been stolen or devoured
The sky is immense and in falling the smallest star would
   frighten your eyes

Paris 1939

In the Glare of the Gestures

Now when bright, anguish turns into thirst
Drought light
Your eyes painful

Renounced vows and black metamorphoses!

Attract contempt by the admission of crimes completely fabricated
Throw yourself in the water drown your gaze in an impure future
Cities sleep under the sea
Nothing belongs to you, neither this hatred nor the reflection of
    our actions
Nothing belongs to you and your sex scares you

The return is made of shadow, silence and water
The return is bold and enlightened
Its magic lost

So who were we to reply 'Turn back'?

Paris 1939

Here Lies the Heart

Like a hunted animal
A ship in distress
A child alone in the night
A stray hour
I wait

I already felt the waves of return
Or have I rushed my life?
In the gap between each rhythm forces intersect
Never again hot or cold pain
You will not live under the pressure of these metamorphoses
Nothing the hands do leaves a trace
Shadows are coming, wherefrom we do not know
Escort and then replace the sand figures
In a world of no return
The order of numbers and stars
A game of chess
Takes place without surprises
But the heart is the measure of chance
Next to us ahead and back
One drowning after another
Love is not made solely of anguish
Like the world or like you
It sometimes relies on some certainty
Or a pebble of blood
Going to you before the eyes
The mouth is already disturbed
At the temple of fear the doors remain open
Then other strange encounters are remembered
To be added and distracting from the signs in my favour

Paris 1939–Lisbon 1940

Very Long Hours

Throw away the misfortunes of the world
I rejected all pain
Mistakes have made my past an indecipherable language

I am no longer afraid

Your hatred does not hurt me anymore
Your grief I feel even more
Distraught by flesh and shadows
A broken heart knows no more what to give

New York 1940

Spartans 1940

Lovers of the Fuhrer
Locked up in iron brothels
Air conditioned with fear
We made you gigolos of death
Paris Place Clichy recognises you
And cries

New York 1940

Unpublished American Poems (1952–1953)

Before the night fades into shadows
and dreams are turned into time
rubies can be black, blood can creep,
and a pool of frogs will gasp for air
while on a bed of bread we choke
evoking pearls imperfect, breasts that are not wine

Way back the sun is reaching for the greyness
of a despair that touches dawn
the simple first hour of yet another day

Corruptions

Veronica! Vera Icona! Mondrian: the image without the veil. Choose the out-of-place; the face in the mirror. We now see through a glass darkly; we now see Medusa. I is another we never see face to face; 'I is another' was darkly said. Darkness and Distance should rhyme; Veronica's veil and Medusa's mirror rhyme. Death is darkness and distance turned into stone, but glass is solid water. The stone should echo; glass should echo images; the stone gong tolls for the death of Narcissus.

Obstacles: altars of delay; delay is the blood of art; art: the ceremony of sacrifice. Only man, coiling and recoiling, knows how to delay satisfaction. The coward turns his back, the artist masks his face, the victim's face is veiled. Witness Bosch's self-portrait, all stone and dampness, hurled into Hell; Watteau's forsaken Gil, all silk and music; Chirico's abandoned jester, all wood and pantomime.

The fool hath said in heart 'there is no pain;' he who says 'God is,' because of pain, is unwise. Because I is another I will wear the fool's mask and gaze at my mother through a mirror. All flesh is grass and the serpent the flower of grass. Now we see through the grass face to face.

New York, April 1952

The Island

Fish, swimming in the sand of dreams, challenge the wind. Anointed with visions, nudists crowd their darkest hour with the fire of lust, the fire of sand, the ice of hearts, with jesters and hard luck. Forsaken canaries peck at the orange peels the sand picked up. Seagulls curve the wind, women curve, boys curl their hair, ship owners curl their lip over a sun-kissed martini and potato chips. Paramours, black with unbelief, idly dial the lemon peel around the bottom of the emptied glass, recalling hour spent in sunken dreams, in shipwrecks of delight while, all along the beach, fishermen curve their rods above the waves.

Togetherness

for Lolya

The mind has not yet reached the lips' laughter.
The eyes sparkle. The soul now loses its shadow. Now, that moment in wanderings when images crack under the lamp's recognition and sound imitates babbling water. Now, the moment when laughter avoids avoiding, when unending searchings are there: in the spreading of vibrations.
Submerged, but dry as shadows, ready to resume the confounding wanderings of the never there, laughter again and again proposes the unheard of to take in at a glance, or refuse out of contempt for the soul and in fear of readiness.
The dryness of laughter in the cool morning air!
The hollowness of laughter at three in the morning!
Oh to be filled with laughter – with your laughter
And exposed to the folly of wanderings!

**Nikitas
Randos
Street
(1963–1977)**

Foreign Vessels

Sayeth Mr Fix to Callirhoe: 'I am the Ilisos river'
sayeth Hilton to the Parthenon: 'I am the Acropolis'
sayeth Edison to the Owl: 'I am the light'
sayeth little Helen to Belafonte: 'You are my Homer.'
As a matter of courtesy Niarchos will be named Navarchos
and its pontoon Tositsas.
The Unknown God became a crossword.
The word be praised that Areopagus remains a rock
and the GB Grande Bretagne instead of Cyprus!

With Kisses

Irma with her peppermint, but whiskey for her customers.
'Excuse me, darling, that was the porter at hotel 'Cairo City'
an American wants me – not tonight, I can't –
I told you so and don't you forget it.
My boy, you didn't tell me your name?'
'And you, when they don't call you Irma?'
'My dear, you want to know everything, don't you?'
'Everything for one night, from mouth to mouth on your whole body.
You were Aspasia and I met you on Pericles Street
with the permanganate. She sent me a postcard from Port Said
the next day the Italians entered Addis Ababa.
Permanganate. I can still see it. A peculiar smell.'
'The whiskey is more expensive.'
'Irma, you are like an inverted rhyme.'
'You want it all, my precious.'
'Pericles' Aspasia was also like that.'
'Come on, I'm in a hurry. The client from 'Cairo City' will be here
    any minute now.'

Heroi(n)sm

Whoever drinks poison, for a little while or for long
kept a place for the priest at the dinner table.
He has Mithridates for a hero!
Touch wood! Whoever administers communion cures
salvation without medication crawls into History
and into its dens, with theatre and heroin,
at the synagogue an audience satiated with love hears Mass.

Man of Two Races

Mrs Pagony from Miami and Pharsala
this year celebrates Greek Easter by dancing
Rock and Roll with a Palace guard
and Mr Pagony, he is also dancing with a Palace guard
while in Plaka, an Englishman with perfect Erasmian pronunciation
recites Cavafy. Mr Stevenson,
originally Stefanakos, spends his summers on the island of Hydra
in a pirate's grand mansion, with leather furniture
of genuine tarpaulin.
Hotel Cyprus Aphrodisia, formerly Angleterre
was overrun by a group of existentialists, worldly non-existent.
Tomorrow they are playing *Hecuba*, dragging with her dance
the Volga Boatman.
We adulterated the honey of Hymettus until it became floor polish
for the tango of the Greeks. We are at a loss
since celebrating Easter at Passover.
Fortunately beer is good for your ethos
fortunately we have Tsitsanis, David and Orpheus.

Storm of Misfortune

A rally. An oil cruise full of old shrews.
A sortie from the position of *Laid up ships*
Libertide to others.
Dr O'Nicey is the talk of the town
with his sibylline 'The Walls of Panama
has bent the lucky walls of Themistocles.'
They accuse him of calling a skiff a ship.
Excavations have brought to light
coins minted by Themistocles
silver-plated and unclaimed.
In a frenzy the crowds cry out
'Down with Wall Street.'
No such luck without walls.
The thread was cut by the storm of misfortune.
The cruise must become a crusade.

'Man of foreign race, how come you dropped anchor in Nova York?'
'This is where Babylon is!' 'And what about Athens, and Paris?'
'They're not yet Venice and lagoons
and if luck should abandon me, I will hold on to my memory
to its Persians, to its Magi and my suns
and wherever I have no memory I shall cast a shadow
words with no breeze, sea shells, exorcisms,
echoes, antichrists! Frenzied drumming
resound within the conches
since I swallowed my modesty in the salty light of the Aegean
and the tempest, I now kiss you Babylon.'

Melina, queen of my Sundays, adieu!
Long-drawn-out songs drag together with your voice
a Mozart serenade. Brothel words tap out the beat of the melody
Lunedí, Martedí, Mercoledí, or Mercury day.
Melina let's go to a secret Ermoupolis
some Saturday night the restlessness will cast anchor
On a Sunday only the poem is observed
it works without emotions, pleasure or pain
to remake words that are hermaphroditic, insulting
inaccessible to record-lovers, beggars, priests, athletes.

Mockery

For Mary Tricherousa
a bouquet of thorns. Long live her bastard son.
Tomorrow we celebrate St Christopher the Dog-Face
The neighbourhood women call little Christ an ugly dog-face.
They have put the evil eye on him! sighs his godmother
They have made him lose his voice! says Josephoglou.
He gets the hiccups when he hears the holy Mass!
science declared.
He was healed though by the priest's wife
with the words of Roidis. Not entirely.
He barks again whenever he reads anthologies of our poets
the flowery words of critics and church calendars.
They respect him though, those who prefer
the anathemas to festivals.

Sweet-Kissing Aspasia

Above Plaka, on the 'Terrace of Pericles'
Cafés like 'Sonia and Loumidis' will photo-sound
three erotic scenes in no time.
Miss Hell-as and Michel Miss-Ellin
will co-operate with 'Mouzika before Bouzika.'
They will grin with smiles.

The Acropolerodion is over-crowded:
The Potter who discovered the poetic worth of warm water
tonight recites 'Mr Baklava is sweeter than death'
as long as the market police have no objection.
They will also be screening *From Hill to Hilton*
inspired by the uphill march
of a female regular reader of the Asbestia.
It is a moving moment when Xenia
calls out: 'Mon Dieu, Mon Dieu, Elpis, *le telephon!*'

Stray priests and spineless cats
rush out from the country chapels
and the neighbourhood grill-houses
chanting 'Oh my, oh my, amen, amen, miaow, miaow.'
And an innovation: in blind alleys
Seferises with their quick taxis
will remove by way of Collisions Avenue
all the broken pieces to crack them with wild enthusiasm.

Happy City

They go to the Rotten Gardens
to revel in the glory of their failure.
The old courtier very patriotically
eats a Danish pastry
while at the neighbouring table
a gipsy woman reminds his son
that in Denmark the statue of the Little Mermaid was beheaded.

But the issue has no poetic acuteness
will the Lady of the Palace give or not give
her annual garden party since
the honourable Lady E.R.E. is no longer in the Ministry of
    Co-ordinated Squeezing
and the director of International Cold Tourism has been dismissed?
Will the Golden Lady swim in the same pool now as leftists?
She better not open her newly built cistern
better she drown! But then what would she gain?
At the Palace, theatricals are frowned upon.
She will somewhat conform to the new state of affairs
and every night before going to the tennis club
she will stroll amongst the common people in Zappeion Park
which, as they say, is full of studs and grabbers
In the meantime
the gipsy woman reminds the leftists to
'Beware of Greeks bearing gifts!'

In the Isles of Byron and Sappho
on the shrinking sands of Greece
Host of heroes and sex
Ladies and gents knee deep in sex
drown their darkest hour
in the lungs of Frank Sinatra
In the courts of nightingales
Moth eaten butterflies
Rock and Roll with Palace guards
Cavafy's city, Pharaoh's Leningrad
are howled and pounded down
with a typewriter Shelley Erotica
in Cretan bar

No and Never

We have our own 'Kifissia,' without trees or greenery
full of bouzoukis, retsina, Greek kids and 'Zorbas'
Instead of the 'Stars' we have the 'Astoria'
We also suffer torments. You suffer tormentors, the Strongmen of the Crown
The junta, Hessa, shit scared mini king and viceroy Maximus
they put an end to all joy. Perverted Pattakos and his pack prattle on like parrots
The Greek flag flaps like a flag of convenience for money together with the junta

Foreign companies work wonders. Morea will turn into Panama
and Hermes become banana and a bonus for tourism
thanks to the cold tourism the Greeks will fast three times a week
and follow a daily diet of morality and censorship
so that Freedom will grow thinner

In the harbour of the free emigrated
a handful of Greeks with Melina and ink
with speeches on paper and records give the junta the finger
thundering out their identity
The 'no' of the Resistance, and the 'never'
of another and one other and yet another young Bouboulina

'There is no answer at three hundred and thirty-three.'
Next door to that number '2 Kriezotos Street.'
The Battle at Issus!
'Miss Pythia, try again.'
'Nikitas Randos, can't you hear me?
Thirty-three was the year of your first poetic attempt'
Twenty-two the year the Greeks returned from Asia Minor.
Oh, return History!
Homer's Troy, the Troy of dreams
triune systems prehistoric, post-Christian
cabalistically calculated.
'Nikitas Randos, why don't you answer?'
Thirty-three years and then The Battle of Echoes returned:
'Don't you recognize me? I am a Manhattanite from Plaka,
and within me shout
the burning visions of your troubled soul.'

We want no absolution.
Down with Nazarene and Viennese peddlers!
What do I have to do with Adam or Oedipus
since I cultivate the enigma?
It is carried from crisis to crisis
a little light from a beam, asterisk of the word
reference to glass powder,
in capsized hours, from the shore and the horizon,
in delights within and without manifestations of agony,
of the shrill E and the big Omega
the difference lies in the sides of a corner in rough seas
Innocent other than the godless?

Past happenings are blooming in the green-houses of hope
Sibyl anthologies, calculation of stars and pleasures
– cheaper in Piraeus –
poets are smugglers of visions
lovers and satirists, card-players shuffling syllables.
The playing of their verse is absolution.

I received the Acropolis from the moon
light my way so I may walk amongst my nightmares
I kiss Judas Iscariot, Morosini and Polybius
instead of the Kore, the Virgin Mother, the Toledo
and the Campaign, the Acropolis stays true.

On the Parthenon on a moonless night tonight the word
let's not forget that Oedipus sought asylum
in Athens, not a kingdom
and now when the Acropolis
has become an immense electrical sacrifice
turn your eyes to Aphrodite.

I engage in allusions and illusions
the space is cultivated
the eyes separate from the belly
the I from you.
The resultant pleasure of image and sonnet
is conveyed with the repetition of the erotic
and the rhythm. It makes the image a body
and the body the embodiment of an image.
How night has fallen since time is missing
the universe passed through me and now
the poem comes closer.
Further that way I see suns not yet set
star of Aphrodite and the ghost of an oracle
for my white verse.

When your heart misses a beat and you catch your breath
evoke the sounds of baroque music
remember also how the baby is lulled to sleep
by the quiet beat of a mother's heart.
Now when your life is breaking down
cardiographs are beeping the dangerous
rhythm of their turmoil
while sending your anxiety to sleep.
I attempt to form a diagnosis of baroque structure.

The fare from Athens to Nova York
how is it calculated? in Babylonian dollars
or in drachmas? How are the images transferred from English
to our language? How is paper money transmuted into metal coins?
The juggling of financiers
will not stop History.
When poetry fails to produce hieroglyphics
it is for records and megaphones. For optical records
the ray of the golden rule. The treasures of the Nile
is now transferred from the land desecrated by Nazarenes
in a boat steered by the glow of Aphrodite.

The Back of the Hare My One and Only Monarchical Love

Our first despots were the Wittel-Vlachs
Otto the Bumpkin with no-brains Amalia. Then
the river Volga spewed up, instead of Aphrodite, Olga the Dirty Romanov
who lavished the Glücksburgs with mittens at an interest
and the Greeks with anathemas.
The cocky son got unwise and conquered Sophia
instead of Constantinople.

One of his sons received the kiss of death from Mr Monkey.
While another paved the silky way for the culture of Metaxas.
Hessa was contriving behind the back of Paul
and King Dunghill II devised utter nonsense with his Anna Maria.

Now the Glücksburgs have to go
and eat their Danish pastry somewhere else
Iranically, perhaps, in lucky Tehran.
Here, perverted Pattakos and his pack of claptrap Strongmen
prattle on like parrots
His Royal Riches
is coming or going to the shits.

Greece of workers and countrymen, Greece of poets
Beware of Greeks. Caution
Defeat or Ready the Tanks.

Bacillicide

I cultivated a closed garden
night blossoms and flowers of cynicism
sweet smell of the abyss, a garden of letters
encloses me, many-coloured, hermetical
chromosomal the word. I torment images
with words that delay them
I recognise differences otherwise the poem won't appear
and place-names and anecdotes return.

Belated and backward dreams stink like cod
long-drawn-out songs from Ioannina and Constantinople
Anatolian songs stink like bonito fish.

Moments scattered on rocks
pine-trees, melon rinds, once in a while
moments sunk in time.
A breath of inspiration in-between the leaves and the sexes.
Lunatic asylum and laurel my world the guts inside me.
I now ask for madness to blunt the paper.

Regime of allusions and precision
or else my poetry stays like that love
which knows no love.
I was enthralled by the anti-poetic
and avoid the lyricism and rhetoric
of delirium.
The poem should offer resistance
the next but one is delayed
we are talking about poetry not creation
nature or metaphysics
we are talking about a regime of uncertainties
about the poetic in-the-meantime.
The future stays behind us. Perhaps
we will have time to engrave
the moment has come.

Structure and breath the poem
flesh of words, tempest of the mind
ray of the super-ego,
the hieroglyphics of yourself.

I add together names
which throw alphabetical dice.
The facts were pushed aside
the reason was lost
I go where I will be.
I tautologise.
Let's dispose of confession
with words and fists.

The wind-swept branches of Pennsylvania
are weaving gossamer words in the sky
in their outline I read the unknown.
An islander soaked in the moonlight of olive trees
revolutionary, emigrant, I profess to be
an interpreter of dreams. I study the Magi
van Eyck and Bosch, Breton
and Duchamp. I greet the atheist Buddhists
of Colorado, anarchists and heretics.
I celebrate the solstices and the anniversary
of every Commune. I venerate the shadow of Mount Athos
the pyramids and Aphrodite.
I lose myself in the crowd and find myself again
in the arteries of Babylon
in the palm of the future.

Manhattan 1977

Scripture
And Light
(1977–1982)

Second Book

Memory is also reflected. My travels,
to Syros from Manhattan,
the new Ermoupolis, is measured.

The speedboat met me with repetitions.
The deck full of flesh with greasing.
Some unfutouristic Hermes the other day charmed
a shipload from the far north: 'An eight-day stay
from Wednesday to Wednesday in Mykonian aphrodisia.'
Clearly without Apollo
the sun shines on pagan bodies.

Mister Head of First Class is going to Tinos
he made a solemn vow. Pale, young, since being cured
of venereal disease, matrimonially he will worship
the Virgin: 'She is the one I adore – don't let me see any priests.'
His pregnant wife and other ladies
despise nudity but not doughnuts.

The Holy Communion is not for me, my superstition
cup of Cycladic civilization: I interpret it
Two-faced Hermes: 'Second account'
Of money and the word. 'Commerce des idées'
as the French say. The transaction of ideas appeal to me.

I returned from Ermoupolis on the same day
Mister Head of First Class failed to return my greeting.
on our going there I had told him that I was an atheist.

With mandolins a troubadour with lovely locks
descending from Saxons captivates us
with the deep grumble of unemployed and vagabonds.

The head of department at Exxon is on leave
in Saudi Arabia. A five hour flight

from Mykonos. In Frisco his Vietnamese wife
is waiting for him.
His brother, less handsome, is travelling with him
A major at the American army unit in Essen
he left his wife in Kassel. Three hours from Glyfada.
Exxcept for the common surname and siren moods
they don't resemble each other at all neither in appearance nor in attitude.
They promised me to visit Ermoupolis
should they return before the end of the year.

Rich island, Syros, with shipyards
and global conferences.
The wheat of Romanian grandfathers
and the cotton of Alexandria
have been replaced by petrol.
Flags of convenience were added
to the second books.
In the years of Turkish rule, was the Catholic Church
not also a flag of convenience?
My Chios-Syros Kalamaris-ink has not yet
dried up. I am ostracized. Drawing up
contracts with demons.

In the glass-covered back of the United Nations
the one and only Ermoupolis is reflected
sails, vans, roll touristically
to the opposite shore of plans and things.
At this hour darkness spreads in the Aegean.
The other day an electric shock erupted here.
The night became night. A night of bewilderment
unreasoning, apocalyptic.

June–July 1977

Kneeling Descendant

An inch of the future I ask of Luck
for my visions. I am a descendant
of the hermaphrodite Adamas and a pupil
of the dark Oedipus.

I met Mrs Perry again, beautiful as always,
elegant, with a steady gait. The right hand
holding on to the dog leash with blind faith. It grew old though
the dog. The husband is quite young. Once in a while
he accompanies her, supporting her arm
with his left hand. He is silent.
She seems to be sexually satisfied.

In a well-known porn-shop two blind couples
fingered erotic objects and sadistic tools
in a crude manner. They will come back again, so they said.

Since Marquis de Sade has replaced Moses
any return of Adam to the heavenly kingdom is out of the question
– paradise of eunuchs and angels.
Only the lover is kneeling
Ethiopian or Belarusian the woman for you
The Song of Solomon!

Falling Stars

Evzone Street, a memory of barracks.
A songbird sat his fear of freedom down
on our fence. I observe the rhythm of its recitation.
Pale white beauty. Lost among the pine-trees of a Byzantine building
victim of a cat or heavenly predatory its sacrifice.
It will not be easily forgotten by our veranda.

Thus the sparrow with the broken wing was remembered
as it sat every afternoon on the same spot
on the telegraph wire. Underlining our boredom
while the yoghurt salesman's voice dragged its way
from the heat of Bachelor's Square.
In the hallway Sœur Irène's slippers mumble
'the doctor will be here any minute now'. Whistling a tune from Larissa.
When are we leaving?

The sun will underline again tomorrow
deep shadows on the southern sides of the cells
disturb the monotony of the pale white wall.
A landscape worthy of de Chirico, poet of momentous incisions.

When will we again see the summit of Mount Kazbek,
the Armenian bell-tower?
Valley of Paulician faiths and communist heresies.
Just like here, so also in Georgia, orthodox traditions
intersect with Ottoman fleecing
Anatolian glances. Struggles, flesh.

We are now the children of a Babylonian Manhattan
tonight we recollect the world of our childhood duties
the philology of ourselves thanks to dialogue
we care for. The word is reinforced, it's reinforced.

Anargyros Petrakis, the first mayor of Athens
is commemorated. In Tbilisi you couldn't find
the grave of your father, a new road
had levelled the big estates, the privileges,
the bold waters of the Kura River were painted in blood.

The poet reveals the spoils of memory
the vicar of facts he plays with the treasures
of a Freudian Mycenae. The shadow of Orestes
clouded over the constellation of Perseus tonight.

In Persia the earth is trembling, medicine men
cook up revolting dishes there.
At Arabat, have pity on the workers, the oil
flows again. When it reaches Salamis Bay
remember the Persians. Admire the falling stars!

Younger because he innovates
exposing freedom to chance
composing equations of metonymies and images
cultivating insomnia to oppose
a mythical blank to the dreams of myths.
He reveals. Substitutes theophany
with the epiphany of the word. Hermaphrodite child
of the prodigal son and mania
Without beginning! He's photographing aspects
of his dark room.

Godless only the Hermaphrodite
in the garden of Letters
'I am the being.' Believing
that good is the disease of
evil
and that it is opposed
by the alchemists of the word
by wandering jugglers
and other vagrants
at one crossing
luck intersects with history
at another with love.
This is how Freedom is born again.

1980

The Day After Yesterday

In my mind. I made a new triune arrangement
of the chairs at Café de la Place Blanche
while waiting for Elisa Breton to come.
I had an urgent need to make a reference
to the 1930s – socialism and surrealism.
Later on I met Elisa at Adami's soiree.
The widow of André Breton
had become entangled in a Gordian knot of cars
at the Left Bank. Wheels or chairs? dilemmas of our time.
The manikins of Masson and Dominguez
lent colour to the opening of the 'Paris-Paris' exhibition
the day after yesterday is hard to connect with the day before tomorrow.

Place Blanche, on a white background the announcement
of those we've lost. The light of heirless iconolaters
how distant my past became when I found out
that Georges Henein had withdrawn from the games of our ideas
'A voice from far away,' answered me
on the phone. A face that faded away before I caught up with him.
How Ionian that Copt was, and I Hellene.
We talked of our ancestors Julian and Trismegistus.

The chairs are empty and it is still too early
for them to be weighed down by a new burden.
Maybe I will pass on the message again under another galaxy.

Manhattan 1982

The Last American Poems (1979–1982)

Black is Beautiful

The Abyssinia I know has not been mapped
objects animated wander right and left
dry bones of camels and their riders
of Pontiacs and their drivers
lie scattered on the deserted grounds.
This is not how Memling envisioned Golgotha
nor how Rimbaud understood the Commune.
The alchemy of images requires that the zero point be black.
I realized it when I was mugged coming out of the 42nd street
    subway station.
Prison bars for dope addicts or a black rose for eros?
This week the manikins of Bonwit Teller, all dressed in black
are more beautiful than ever. The blind man brought by limousine
to beg before elegant shop windows reminds me that
the Canaitish woman was a dog. Water was turned into wine
by a descendant of Solomon and his black queen
a visionary and forerunner of Malcolm X
in the temple of the Pharisees bow low before an oil painting
of squares not black enough for black.
In the Red Square Lenin lies mummified.
Abyssinia travels into my past.
Through underground channels I will escape from Athens
bankrupt and tourist ridden. My destination: Addis Ababa.
He was the first journalist to announce the flight of the Emperor
and lived off this scoop for ever after.
Not so the young Ethiopians who to avoid being enrolled in
    Mussolini's fascist brigades
were whisked out of the country to feed the black market of
    hermaphrodite flesh.
Walking idly on the Rue du Dragon the Greek asked the Ethiopian
what was the common denominator between the labyrinth and the
    spider.

Four o'clock

From a mountain peak Manfred – or was it Gilgamesh? –
   glided to a landing place south of Boulder.
Without Byron and Zarathustra, perhaps also Rousseau, the Alps
   would have remained a footpath for Hannibals, Bonapartes and
   Saint Bernards.
Without gods, admittedly a tiresome lot, Mount Olympus would
   never have risen above nature.
Prometheus, the master potter, might still be stewing his vultures in
   Caucasian wines.
Nowadays we take it for granted that the world is neither supported
   by Atlas nor by a cross bearing Nazarene.

A Himalayan vision unbound rocky mountains of Tibet and
   Colorado.
For urbanites the world is a theatre scooped in the flank of a hill or
   impressed on the mind by a volcanic explosion of Nietzschean
   proportions.

Circles within circles magnetize sounds, electrify clouds and caves.
   From where comes the voice and the echo from where? More
   powerful than stillness is immobility. Bound to language mind is
   unlocked by ecstasy and rocked by breath. Apparitions carried by
   the wind of crevasses bounce back and forth against unwritten
   mountain tablets. Stones tremble. The wild cat blinks.

Not for me the Himalayas and the sanctuaries of émigré llamas.
I'm attuned to the school of worldly upheavals and to the fusion of terror and beauty.
But I'm haunted by the shadow of Mount Athos.
Triangular, I still see it dialling midnight at sunset.
On the road to Aurora I perceived that the twenty fifth hour of the day is disrupting the summer solstice.
Pressing my hand against my heart I noticed that it had missed a beat.
At that precise moment a young woman with Mongolian chromosomes asks me 'how far are we from four o'clock?'

Who Speaks?

Did your eyes cross swords with your mother's?
And did the mirror break you? Who speaks?
The fool who said 'nothing is' or the other who says 'there is nothing'?
Who speaks? Images were given to us the way trees were given
    the wind and the rocks running water.
From the subdivision of visions where do we go?
I believe that which is absurd. Athens or Jerusalem?
The voice of the owl stuck in my throat. The road to Moscow was
    blocked.
Paris, the Mystic Babylon. 'We shall transform the world and
    regenerate ourselves.'
Jeanne D'Arc is dead, 'Vive Violette Nozière' Violette who?
Once again ink flows in my veins and I can look with astonishment
    into the eyes of others
of the woman with the Spanish laughter framed by the first wrinkle of
    sorrow
of the Nordic with the stage voice and the too silent audience
of the Berliner stroking her cheek with the caress of a dove while
    plotting the death of Hitler
I gazed into the eyes of young poets with their dreams of incest and
    chocolate guillotines.
Tomorrow we celebrate the death of Louis XVI. We shall send a
    letter to Leon Trotsky.

Refugees from Spain pour into France. The City of Potters with
    its Maginot Line dreams of umbrellas and telephone calls.
Now comes the exodus – of Picasso's paintings, of the mistress of a
    Balkan king
of the antifascist poet and the Freudian analyst.
Wanderer, what is your destination: Jerusalem or Babylon?

I am for the city of towering towers, of streets like canyons
I am for dreams of five cent cigars that taste like Wall Street
of electric chairs with the smell of van Gogh, of giant
    hamburgers atop Hamburger Hill, of mushrooms taller than Hiroshima
of a paradise as big as a refrigerator and with enough gold to armour
    the teeth from the cold of ice cream.
I am for birds with too many leaves and for trees with too many
    feathers. I am for Manhattan and Satan, for the Mad Hatter and
    Lucifer, for a voice that comes from the Steppes, for my Moonbeam,
    murmuring sweet things with Russian vowels and Georgian
    consonants, for the trust and doubt in her loving eyes in the game I
    was to play after, during and after the Revolution.

On the alchemy of words, of beauty and the beast, the confrontation
    of love and will, the complexity of the Sphinx and Oedipus.
The fool hath said in his heart, that is secretly, and metaphorically,
    'there is no truth.'
Beyond Oedipus and Freud there is the riddle, the searching eyes,
    the veil of Ambiguity and enchantment
the magic of surprise.

Xmas = 125th Street

Never have my ears recognised the taste of my voice
my mouth does not see poetry and my expectations count and
    recount the gaps
Keep moving between Columbus Avenue and Third Avenue
The telephone keeps ringing surrealist reminiscences
On One Hundred and Twenty Second Street I begin counting the bones
for the hospital of bone diseases while a harlot screams her lost past
The Russian Church migrated to better quarters
what am I doing measuring repetitions and fractionalising distances
Is this still now a lyrical motif? Astrologers have forgotten the Nativity
All that I ask for is to remain a stranger wherever I happen to be
My next observations will probably take me to 8th Street
So many who were there count no more; add salt to your tears
and invectives to your keys.

Notes

Acropolis
Ioannis Psycharis (1854–1929) was a French philologist of Greek origin, author and promoter of Demotic Greek (the modern vernacular form of the Greek language) who lived most of his life in Paris. Fred Boissonnas (1858–1946) was a Swiss photographer famous for his travel images of Greece, and especially his studies of the Acropolis 1900–1922. Ernest Renan (1823–1892) was a French philosopher and writer known in Greece mainly as the author of the text 'Prayer on the Acropolis.' Karl Baedeker (1801–1859) was the founder of a German publishing house famous for its guidebooks; four travel guides to Greece and Athens were produced between 1889 and 1909. The Zappeion Hall is a building in the National Garden in central Athens used as a conference and exhibition centre. Francesco Morosini (1618–1694), the Doge of Venice, was in command of a fleet against the Ottomans at the time of the outbreak of the Morean War. During the siege of Athens in 1687 his artillery caused great damage to the Parthenon, and he oversaw the looting of many of the surviving sculptures.

Foreign Vessels
Karolos Fix was a Greek industrialist who made a fortune from Fix Beer. Callirhoe is a mythical ocean nymph and also the name of a large street in Athens. Ilisos is a river in ancient Greece which has now been largely canalized into underground routes around Athens. Niarchos derives from 'nia', a Homeric word for ship and 'archos' (leader) and is a pun on the famous ship owner Stavros Niarchos. *Navarchos* (Miaoulis) was a great Greek cruiser, launched in 1879, which was purchased as a part of the naval expansion after the unsuccessful Cretan uprising in 1866. Michael Tositsas was a Greek-Egyptian businessman and entrepreneur who, together with his wife Eleni, became important benefactors to Greek institutions. Areopagus (Hill of Ares) was in ancient Greece a hill in Athens on which was sited the highest governmental council and later a judicial court; today it stands for the Supreme Court of Appeal. 'Grande Britagne instead of Cyprus' is a direct reference to the Cyprus situation since several establishments with English names in Greece

were, for a short time, hurriedly renamed 'Cyprus' during demonstrations against Britain in the mid-1950s.

With Kisses
Cairo City was the name of a hotel in Athens in the early 1950s. It is also a reference to Egypt and its relationship to Britain which here is likened to the Greek–English problem of the same period because of the Cyprus crisis. Potassium permanganate can be used as a disinfectant; it was also used to self-induce abortions; both usages were common among prostitutes at the time. Fascist Italy invaded Ethiopia in 1935. In Greek, the word for rhyme is spelled 'rima' – an anagram of 'Irma'. Aspasia (470–400 BC) was famous for being involved with the Athenian statesman and general Pericles. She was rumoured to have been a brothel keeper and a harlot.

Heroi(n)sm
Mithridates the Great was a king of Pontus (120–63 BC) who slowly habituated himself to the use of poison so as to ward off a possible attempt on his life by poisoning.

Man of Two Races
Vasilis Digenis Akritas was a tenth-century Byzantine hero; his father was a Muslim and his mother a Christian Greek. 'Pagony' means peacock in Greek. 'Erasmian pronunciation' is a system of pronouncing ancient Greek devised by Erasmus. During the 19th century many Hydra islanders became pirates after refugees flooded the island. Great fortunes were thus begun and some of these pirates even brought architects from Venice to build palatial houses. During the Cyprus crisis of the mid-1950s many English-titled hotels in Athens temporarily changed names as a comment on the British rule of the island. *Hecuba* is a tragedy by Euripides. The Greek Fix Beer invented the slogan that 'it is good for you.' Vasilis Tsitsanis (1915–84) was a popular composer, singer and bouzouki player.

Storm of Misfortune
The foundations of many Greek shipping fortunes lay in the purchase of US Liberty ships after the Second World War.
Dr O'Nicey' is a pun on the Greek shipping magnate Aristotle Onassis. Themistocles was an Athenian statesman who was instrumental in

building up the Athenian fleet. He also built the defensive walls running from Athens to Piraeus.

Melina, queen of my Sundays, adieu!
The actress Melina Mercouri was most famous for her portrayal of a prostitute in the film *Never on Sunday* (1960). Ermoupolis is the capital of the island Syros which is a junction for boats in the Cyclades, the Greek island group in the Aegean Sea.

Mockery
Mary Tricherousa is the name of a miracle-producing icon on Mount Athos in which the Holy Virgin is depicted with three hands. Godmother means the mother of God rather than a traditional godmother. The religious writer Fotis Kondoglou tried to revive the traditional art of icon-painting. Emmanuel Roidis (1836–1904) was excommunicated from the Greek orthodox Church for writing the comic novel *Pope Joan*. The female name Evanthia denotes the holy women of the Greek Orthodox Church, and derives from the ancient word for flowery or blossoming.

Sweet-Kissing Aspasia
Aspasia was the wife of Pericles. Her name also contains a double pun in Greek 'aspasmos' (kiss or hug) and 'spasimo' (break or crack). Miss-Ellin is a double pun meaning both a hater of Greece and a male whore. The 'potter' refers to the poet George Seferis who received the Nobel Prize in Literature the year this was written in 1963. The motif of the jar or the 'dry pitcher', symbolizing emptiness, was used in several of Seferis's poems, most importantly in 'The King of Asini'. The 'warm water' is a reference to an untitled couplet by George Seferis from 1940 ('The warm water reminds me each morning / that I have nothing else alive near me'). In Greek mythology Elpis was the personification of hope, depicted as a young woman carrying flowers in her hands. Seferis who famously sought inspiration in the 'broken pieces' of mythology and antiquity. 'Collisions Avenue' is a pun on a well-known poem by Seferis entitled 'Syngrou Avenue 1930' and the Greek word for collisions ('syngrousis').

Happy City
The title is a pun on the Danish Glücksburg royal dynasty ruling Greece. The Rotten Gardens refers to the big park in central Athens called Zappeion. The park turns 'rotten' by misspelling Zappeion (Sapion means 'rotten' in Greek). The statue of the Little Mermaid in Copenhagen was

beheaded in 1964, by unknown assailants. In September of the same year Constantine II married Anne-Marie, the Danish princess and sister to the future queen of Denmark, Margrethe. Kostas Karamanlis was the leader of the conservative National Radical Union (E.R.E.) which initially enjoyed the support of the palace but later clashed with Queen Frederica. Fraudulent elections, manipulations and army pressures eventually caused Karamanlis' downfall in 1963 when George Papandreou's Centre Union took over. 'Beware of Greeks bearing gifts!' is a warning to the leftists to be aware of collaborating with the political opposition, even within the ranks of the Centre Union Party, since the party included many right-wing elements.

In the isles of Byron and Sappho

The 'nightingales' is a reference to George Seferis' poem 'Eleni'. The 'moth eaten butterflies' could also refer to one of Seferis' sixteen haikus (1940) where he raises 'a dead butterfly without make-up'. Cavafy's city was Alexandria in Egypt. Nasser was known at the time as Egypt's modern Pharaoh. The phrase 'pounded down' is a pun referring to pound as a unit of weight as well as to the pound sterling, that is, the British-led tripartite attack against Egypt in 1956. 'Cretan bar' is a reference to the British undermining of Alexandria since the first volume of Lawrence Durrell's 'Alexandria Quartet' was written while the author lived on Crete as well as giving prominence to Cavafy.

No and Never

Kifissia is one of the more prestigious northern suburbs of Athens. The Astoria neighbourhood in Queens, New York is known for being home to one of the largest concentrations of Greeks outside Greece. The 'strongmen of the crown' is a reference to the Colonels (Stylianos Pattakos, George Papadopoulos and Nikolaos Makarezos) who ruled Greece from 1967 to 1974. 'Hessa' refers to Queen Frederica through a triple pun which combines the Greek verb for shit (hese), the German royal house of Hessen and an allusion to her murky past as a member of the Nazi youth party in Germany (Rudolf Hess). Her son, King Constantine II was by many seen to be the puppet of his strong-willed mother (thus 'mini'). He was 'shit scared' after a failed counter-coup which saw him flee the country in December 1967 after initially having been involved with the junta. Viceroy Maximus is a reference to general George Zoitakis who served as a regent of Greece from December 1967 until 1972 when he was replaced by the junta leader Papadopoulos. The nickname 'Maximus' is an ironic comment on both the kingdom and the junta by using the Latin term for 'greatest'. The name also refers to the banker and right-wing politician Demetrios Maximos. Morea stands for Greece here (and contains a pun on the Greek word for stupidity 'moria' and 'Morias' meaning the Peloponnese) The reference to Panama suggests that Greece was in effect a US colony. Student revolts in the Panama Canal Zone in 1964 had provoked the violent suppression by American police forces which resulted in many deaths and hundreds of wounded. 'The harbour of the free emigrated' refers to New York and is a pun on the poem 'The Free Besieged' by the national poet Dionysios Solomos. The actress Melina Mercouri was a leading figure in the resistance work of Greeks abroad. Laskarina Bouboulina (1771–1825) was a heroine of the Greek War of Independence in 1821.

'There is no answer at three hundred and thirty-three'
Pythia was a high priestess of the Temple of Apollo at Delphi more commonly known as the Oracle of Delphi. To 'do the Pythia' in Greek also means to speak in a confused manner and not give a straight answer to a question. 'Triune systems' is a reference to Calas' pseudonyms during the 1930s (M. Spieros, Nikitas Randos and Nicolas Calas). Plaka is the Athenian old town.

I received the Acropolis from the moon
King Polybius was the step-father to Oedipus in the famous myth.

The Back of the Hare My One and Only Monarchical Love
King Otto, from the Bavarian house of Wittelsbach, was the first modern king of Greece in 1832. Queen Olga's publication of a translation of the New Testament into modern Greek from the learned diction Koine in 1901, without the authorization of the Holy Synod, led to deadly riots in Athens and the eventual fall of the government of George Theotokis as well as the resignation of Procopius, the Metropolitan Archbishop of Athens. Constantine I supported the Great Idea, aimed at reclaiming Constantinople, which led to the catastrophic war against Turkey in 1922 and the loss of the Greek cities in Asia Minor. King Alexander died from blood poisoning after being bit by his pet monkey. George II supported the

military putsch of the Fascist Ioannis Metaxas in 1936. The wife of King Paul, Queen Frederica was known for her strong will and independence. King Constantine II initially had close connections with the Colonels but his later aborted counter-coup forced him to flee the country. The Colonels were known for endless speeches and ridiculous declarations. The rallying cry of the moderate left was 'Karamanlis or tanks' which plays on the Spartan command telling the soldiers going to war to either win the battle or be carried back home upon their shield.

I cultivated a closed garden
The belated and backward dreams refer to the dream of the Great Idea and the taking back of Constantinople which resulted in the catastrophe of 1922. The Greek word for bonito fish is 'palamida' which is a pun on the name of Palamas.

Second Book
Calas' grandfather Nikolas Kalamaris originated from the island of Chios, but was born on Syros and went on to build a fortune in shipping and import of cotton from Egypt and export of wheat while residing in Romania. Kalamaris-ink is a pun on his original surname which also means squid in Greek.

Falling Stars
Agamon Square is now called American Square (Plateia Amerikis) 'Agamon' means bachelor or unmarried in Greek.

Acknowledgements

The unpublished American poems, 1952–1953, are taken from the Nicolas and Elena Calas Archive at Athens just as the 1960's poem 'In the Isles of Byron and Sappho' which was first published in 2008 ('The critical poetry of Nicolas Calas: challenging the poetics of Greekness' by Lena Hoff in *Byzantine and Modern Greek Studies*, vol. 32:1). 'No and Never' was first published in the *Journal of Modern Greek Studies* ('A Pyrotechnic of Multiple Puns: Decoding the Political Satires of Nicolas Calas' by Lena Hoff, vol. 28:2, 2010). 'Black is Beautiful' was first published in *Beatitude* (vol. 29, Fall 1979), while 'Four O'clock' and 'Who Speaks' belong to the Nicolas and Elena Calas Archive and were first published in *Nicolas Calas and the Challenge of Surrealism*. 'X-mas = 125th Street' is also taken from the archives and is published here for the first time. The previously unpublished poems, as well as the cover photo, are all taken from the Nicolas and Elena Calas Archive at Athens and appear here with permission from the Nordic Library at Athens and Louisiana Museum of Modern Art in Humlebæk, Denmark.